GANG WARS
ON THE COSTA

GANG WARS
ON THE COSTA

THE TRUE STORY OF THE BLOODY
CONFLICT RAGING IN PARADISE

WENSLEY CLARKSON

JOHN BLAKE

Published by John Blake Publishing Ltd,
3 Bramber Court, 2 Bramber Road,
London W14 9PB, England

www.johnblakepublishing.co.uk

First published in paperback in 2009

ISBN: 978 1 84454 808 8

British Library Cataloguing-in-Publication Data:
A catalogue record for this book is available from the British Library.

Design by www.envydesign.co.uk

Printed in the UK by CPI William Clowes Beccles NR34 7TL

1 3 5 7 9 10 8 6 4 2

Papers used by John Blake Publishing are natural, recyclable products made from
wood grown in sustainable forests. The manufacturing processes conform to the
environmental regulations of the country of origin.

Every attempt has been made to contact the relevant copyright-holders,
but some were unobtainable. We would be grateful if the appropriate
people could contact us.

To dear old 'Jungle Bill'

Just keep running, mate. They'll never catch you.

CONTENTS

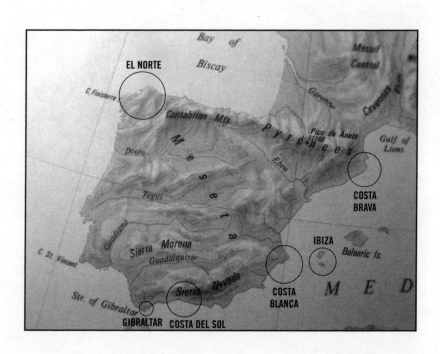

FOREWORD

SPAIN IS PLAYING host to a new breed of criminal from the UK these days. Younger, flashier gangsters have been gradually eroding the power of Britain's traditional criminal families out on the Costa. Many of these characters have settled in Spain. They stay mainly in the background as fixers and organisers, hiding behind legitimate businesses and arranging the links for big drug consignments and all sorts of other crimes.

Drug investigations take up 70 per cent of police work on Spain's coastal regions. And according to Spanish detectives, the typical British and foreign gang leader these days is in his late twenties or thirties. They are the sorts of characters who'll walk into a bar or club and shoot someone to send out a message to rivals: *Don't fuck with me.*

The British gangs in Spain are usually early school leavers with convictions back in the UK, which often gives them status with other criminals who turn to them for help.

These gangs often number 15 to 20 hard core members, some of whom may have grown up together. Violence can flare up when there is a 'crossover' such as a turf war or when a drugs consignment goes missing. Back in the eighties these organised criminals would have turned to armed robbery and then to drugs after building contacts in Spain, South America and North Africa. But since the 1990s they've gone straight into the drugs trade. Back then in Spain, they often invested in the burgeoning club scene and supplied synthetic drugs from Europe, especially Holland. These gangs would protect their territory with sawn-off shotguns and even hired hitmen to send out the 'right' messages.

The sheer number of drug busts in Spain underlines the role being played by British and Irish criminals. In recent years, gang bosses have cultivated their contacts in Spain and set up members of their own gangs to act as international go-betweens with drug smugglers. Those links with Spain have become even more sophisticated and their networks of suppliers and distributors are often now second to none.

Many Irish criminals fled their home country and headed for Spain after the authorities introduced the Proceeds of Crime legislation and set up the Criminal Assets Bureau following the shocking cold-blooded murder of Dublin journalist Veronica Guerin in the mid-1990s. One infamous suspect, known to the Irish police (the Garda) as 'Chaser', is now rated as one of the biggest suppliers of drugs in Europe. This follows the arrest in Spain two years ago of an even more powerful gangster, who was born in Birmingham to Irish parents. After that arrest, 'Chaser' became the Mr Big in Irish drug circles on the European mainland and he has spent the past three years moving between the Netherlands, Belgium and Spain.

Cannabis remains the most widely used drug in Spain. Vast

shipments arrive from North African countries and are also smuggled out of Spain – mainly as freight – on lorries travelling across the continent through France and then on to the UK and Ireland. Until recently, ecstasy was second to cannabis in the market as distribution of the tablets spread to all four Spanish provinces. But in recent years cocaine has overtaken 'E'. It is relatively easy to get a plentiful supply of, and these days it's popular across a broader spectrum of society.

Spain leads Europe for cocaine seizures and it accounts for half of all drug confiscations – and the traffickers are always coming up with new smuggling tricks. Among current techniques are those involving gangs that drop loads of cocaine fitted with radio-transmitting buoys into the Atlantic and have boats pick up the drugs.

But Spain's fast track to a recession has moved the spotlight back on this country's spectacular ten-year building boom, much of which has been driven by 'dirty money'. Criminals capitalised on the gold rush mentality that infected Spain in the 1990s. With house prices doubling in ten years between 1997 and 2007, many were desperate to grab a piece of the action. Some unscrupulous local authorities even turned a blind eye to 'front' companies set up by gangsters and also took backhanders to grant building licences.

Keen to hide the spoils from prostitution, extortion and drug dealing, organised criminals have channelled hundreds of millions of euros into buying property. Meanwhile, police and judicial authorities were often overwhelmed by the scale and sophistication of criminal activities. On the Costa del Sol –

where estate agents believed in the boom years they virtually had a licence to print money – anti-corruption magistrates found themselves dealing with scores of cases.

But then 'dirty' – or undeclared – money has always been something of a national custom in Spain. During property deals, the real value is never declared to the tax authorities. Instead, envelopes stuffed full of cash are passed between buyer and seller, while the notary or lawyer witnessing the transaction conveniently leaves the room. Just how much 'dirty money' entered Spain in those boom years is impossible to say. But it is claimed that 40 per cent of all the € 500 bills in existence are circulating in Spain. They are called 'Bin Ladens' because, like the world's most wanted man, although everyone knows what they look like, no one has ever actually seen one. These € 500 bills fill the envelopes in 'black money' property deals.

Spain became a popular destination for Britons on the run after the collapse of the extradition treaty between the two countries in 1978. But Britain has had an extradition treaty with Spain since 1985, when the country joined the European Union. Yet this has done nothing to stem the tide of gangsters flooding on to Spain's vast coastline. In January 2004 European arrest warrants also came into effect, making it far easier to bring British criminals back into the British criminal justice system. But still they kept coming.

Today it is estimated that the Spanish Costas (meaning coasts) are home to more than 20,000 foreign criminals of

70 nationalities, including the Russian Mafia and armed gangs from Albania, Kosovo and the former Soviet republics. The Costa del Sol was nicknamed the 'Costa del Crime' back in 1983 when the thieves behind London's notorious £6 million Security Express robbery were spotted leading luxurious lives on the Spanish coast. In addition to drugs there is a flourishing trade in illegally imported tobacco and cigarettes, which are almost as profitable to British criminals in Spain as drugs, with minimal risks.

The sums at stake are huge. Officially, one in five cigarettes smoked in Britain has been smuggled into the country, meaning that there is a vast illegal market available to British gangs based in Spain. Unofficially, the figure could be as high as one in three. A packet of 20 cigarettes legally costing more than five pounds a pack can be bought on the black market for half that sum. So smuggling is well worthwhile, with such bootleg trade costing the Exchequer more than £3 billion every year.

There is an ever-growing 'white van' trade on cross-Channel ferries and many people smuggle goods on flights from Spain and the Canary Islands. But 80 per cent of the shipments are by organised gangs operating much like major import-export companies. One 40-foot shipping container can hold up to eight million cigarettes, with a revenue value of £1 million. Consignments pass through the docks mixed with garden furniture and other such legitimate cargos.

Importers can clear a profit of up to £500,000 per container, depending on how many middlemen are involved. The cigarettes end up on sale in pubs and clubs, at car-boot sales and on housing estates. HM Revenue & Customs seize more than a billion illegal cigarettes every year.

However, officials probably only intercept about 10 per cent of smuggled loads. This suggests that up to 10 billion cigarettes are entering the UK illegally.

Unlike trafficking in drugs, there are no steep penalties to deter the black marketeers. The worst they can expect is confiscation and up to seven years in prison, although that is very rare. These 'businessmen' write off a certain percentage of their imports to seizures. They simply buy more cigarettes – which means more orders for manufacturers.

In 2000, the then British Home Secretary, David Blunkett, finalised a new fast-track extradition treaty with the Spanish authorities, but it seems to have done little to stem the tide of crime rolling across Spain. The treaty was supposed to be aimed at figures such as the 'Pimpernel', a multimillionaire criminal who has been on the run for more than 20 years and is believed to be one of the most senior figures in the British underworld.

Spain's criminal gangs undoubtedly benefit from the country's massive 4,900km of coastline, from which drugs shipments can be received from South America, via Morocco or Algeria to the south, and launched into northern Europe, with little fear of detection by police or coastguard patrol boats. Spain's position as a staging post for drugs from places such as Colombia and Bolivia is also partly a symptom of its colonial past and the language ties between Spain and South America.

One of the most disturbing things about researching this book is the way in which Spain has embraced all the luxuries that we take so much for granted but is now on the verge of returning to its previous Third World status. The economy there is even more shattered than that of the UK. Two million properties remain un-lived in because the building boom has flooded Spain with unwanted housing.

Spain is already well into its first official recession in 15 years – 1.3 million workers lost their jobs in 2008, bringing the jobless total up to 3.2 million. At the time of writing, Spain has the highest unemployment rate in the EU at 13.9 per cent, and it is expected to top the 16 per cent mark by the end of 2009.

So there you have it. A brief insight into why Spain has become the gateway to villainy for so many British and Irish gangsters in recent years. Throw into that mix a large sprinkling of criminals from other countries across the globe and it's little wonder that Spain has become a tinderbox of crime, on the verge of exploding at any given moment.

PROLOGUE

HE PULLED THE matt-black Glock automatic out of the glove compartment of the rental BMW and pointed it straight at me, and then a broad smile came over his horribly scarred face. 'This is my favourite toy. With this no one fucks with me. I am the king.' Jimmy's grin exposed two gold front teeth and his piercing blue eyes glistened in the Marbella sunshine. The most frightening thing about having a gun shoved in your face, even jokingly, is looking at the shooter's finger on the trigger, and Jimmy was literally stroking it as he held it up in my direction.

But I could hardly complain. Liverpool gangster Jimmy had taken time out to talk me about the activities of his gang and many of his rivals on the Costa del Sol. The British boys had been given a right hammering by the eastern Europeans on the Costa del Crime in recent weeks. Waving that Glock in my face was part of Jimmy's chilling 'performance' as a criminal face. But it's that very 'performance' by so many criminals now based in Spain that is costing hundreds of people their lives every year. As I discovered travelling the length and breadth of this beautiful country, these gangs murder their rivals because it's part of their business. A well-publicised killing sends out a message to competitors not to overstep the mark. In a sense, it's highly effective PR. And right in the middle of all this murder and mayhem are a lot of Brits like Jimmy.

It was while making a TV documentary with Jimmy about crime in Spain that I came up with the idea for this book. His cold-blooded attitude and the way he has thrived in the all-year-round heat of southern Spain seemed indicative of the way that criminals have flourished in the country for the past 30 years. It's as if it's still the same safe haven it once was. Yet extradition is an everyday occurrence in Spain today, although criminals from all over the world still make it their base because it's easier to operate with impunity in Spain than anywhere else in Europe. It also happens to be the gateway to Africa and South America, sources for 90 per cent of all the drugs that flood Europe every day.

Jimmy operates on the 20-mile strip of coastline between Fuengirola and Marbella. Drugs and prostitution are his main source of income. Narcotics alone are a massive billion-dollar industry in this area. There is a vicious turf war going on between gangs of criminals from the UK, South America, eastern Europe and the former Soviet republics. It's a war that began back in the so-called 'good old days' of the seventies and early eighties, when British villains fled to Spain to avoid extradition.

Muscular and physically extremely fit, Jimmy had the name of a girlfriend tattooed on his left hand. His dark mop of hair and young-looking face belied his 39 years. And despite waving that gun at me earlier, he seemed to have an easy-going manner. He spoke English and Spanish but talked about murdering people as if it was as normal as eating scrambled eggs for breakfast. If he hadn't become a criminal, he told me, he'd probably have been an accountant. His own brother was one. Although he did later let slip that another brother back in Toxteth was a hitman, who occasionally flew over to Spain to carry out jobs for his gang.

Jimmy lived in a penthouse apartment close to the centre of Marbella, overlooking the stunning promenade. Even during the current property price meltdown, it had to be worth half a million pounds. Jimmy had at least a hundred grand's worth of gold jewellery on his fingers and around his neck. He drove rented BMWs, he explained, because he liked to change cars every couple of weeks for 'security reasons'. Jimmy claimed he'd been stabbed five times, which was why he always carried a gun. He had a four-inch scar running from just below his eye to his chin; it contorted whenever he tried to make a point while talking.

Jimmy had spent, he said, ten years of his life in prison and insisted he'd rather commit suicide than ever go back to jail. He made a point of sliding the tip of his own forefinger across his neck to emphasise the point. Then he lifted up the Polo shirt he wore to show me four scars across his stomach. On one occasion, he explained to me in a very cool fashion, he'd lost four pints of blood and almost had his liver punctured. 'They wanted me dead,' he explained. 'Who?' I asked calmly. 'The fuckin' Russians,' he spat. 'I hate them more than other race in the world. They are evil.' Coming from this man it sounded almost incredulous that he could consider other people to be even more evil than himself.

Jimmy was without doubt one of the coldest people I have ever met. But then his coldness probably helped get him through the riskier aspects of his dangerous 'profession'. He never seemed fazed by anything and remained totally focused throughout our meeting. But as we walked along the promenade near his home, his eyes darted up to examine every single face going past us. He never seemed to lose concentration. Even as he talked to me he was actively looking in all directions, just in case anyone tried to have a pop at him.

While I was interviewing Jimmy, his Romanian girlfriend Sasha turned up at the penthouse. She seemed flustered and worried about Jimmy and kept fussing around him. I could see he was getting irritated with her. Then suddenly he grabbed her by the wrist and pulled her off to an adjoining room. Less than two minutes later, I heard her scream and then start sobbing. Jimmy reappeared rubbing his hands together almost gleefully. 'That bitch was out all last night,' he said. 'If I find out who she's fuckin', I'll slit his throat.' Moments later, he returned to his favourite subject – himself.

Jimmy was just one of many criminals I encountered while writing this book but he is undoubtedly a classic example of the crime outbreak that is sweeping the coastlines of Spain. As a veteran true-crime writer, I have come across many notorious gangsters in the past, but what makes Jimmy so important is that he represents a complete sea change in the way villains operate in Spain. These evil, cold-blooded characters take no prisoners. They shoot to kill in a way that has even terrified some of the most infamous British villains of the past. Those old boys of crime say the rules have changed. Women, children and so-called 'civilians' are no longer off-limits to these ruthless characters.

I was deeply perturbed by what I witnessed in Spain during my research into this book. But in order to unravel the truth about this disturbing crime wave, I have had to delve deep into the underworld at considerable personal risk. I am fascinated by how the criminals seem to thrive right under the noses of the police. I've even been inside some of Spain's prisons, where conditions are appalling even when compared to the oldest British jails. I've spent countless hours with killers, drug barons, pimps, child prostitution dealers, counterfeiters, con men and bank robbers. At times I have been threatened, and what I've witnessed has deeply disturbed me, but sometimes I have found myself sharing a beer and a joke with people like the hitman responsible for the deaths of dozens of people who admitted he didn't sleep well at night. This book doesn't set out to answer any questions. It simply lays out the facts and asks you, the reader, to take a journey inside this frightening world. Crime gangs are not a new problem, but their membership does seem to be on the increase, especially in Spain.

I have travelled to all the coastlines, and the holiday islands, of this complex nation and discovered types of criminals I never thought existed. I hope that this book will at least provide you with an insight into a criminal phenomenon that seems to thrive right in the heart of a country visited by more Brits than any other nation on earth and lived in by more than half a million other former-UK residents.

COSTA DEL SOL

Gangsters' Paradise: the view from one gang lord's apartment in Puerto Banus on the Costa del Sol

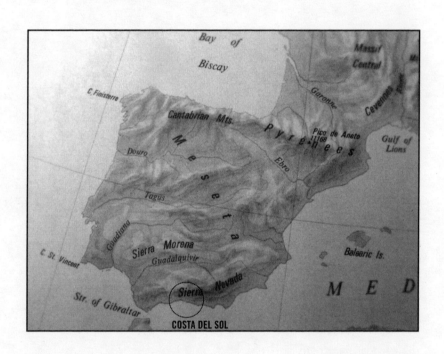

1

ALHAURÍN PRISON IS a foul-smelling hole of a place. The waft of sweat, fear and loathing hits you in the face the moment you walk through the gates. Everything is off-white in colour, from the deadpan faces of the guards to the chipped walls and the yellowing metalwork of the gated doorways. It's a strangely muted place, though, which is surprising because just 50 metres from the entrance are housed about 1500 of Spain's most notorious criminals, merely a few kilometres from Europe's number-one holiday destination.

Alhaurín sits just beneath a vast mountain range, which overshadows the Costa del Sol and is rumoured to contain more shallow graves of dead criminals than any other mountain range in the world. It's what they call a modular prison, which means that there are five different blocks that house different classifications of prisoners; perhaps more surprisingly, there is even a women's block, although the men and women's sections of this prison are not directly connected for obvious reasons.

One British criminal who spent many months in Alhaurín told me that the inmates reckoned the authorities deliberately house the women just within sight so that 'we really suffer'. He said that it was possible to wave to the women in their cells and that sometimes inmates managed to form some kind of long distance relationship, but it all sounds very frustrating and simply adds to the tinderbox atmosphere inside Alhaurín.

From a distance, the prison itself looks like a load of run-down 1970s low-rise tower blocks, right slap-bang in the middle of a desolate rocky terrain looking down towards the sea and the mass of concrete that makes up the Costa del Sol. When Alhaurín was first built, most of the coastal resorts were nothing more than fishing villages dotted along a picturesque, deserted coastline. Now the Costa del Sol looks like a sprawling mini-Rio de Janeiro dominated by bland tower blocks and depressing-looking estates of private holiday homes, jerry-built at high speed during the boom years of the 1990s.

Inside Alhaurín, the grim-faced guards search all visitors in a casual, nonchalant manner, which belies the sort of security one would expect inside the biggest prison in all of Andalucia. These 'screws' seem deadened by the sheer flatness of the atmosphere that pervades in this bland environment. They are poorly paid, and it shows.

I was in Alhaurín to meet Joey, one of the most notorious and well-known British criminals on the Costa del Sol. He'd been arrested a few weeks earlier while dropping off a shipment of drugs at the home of another criminal who happened to be under police surveillance because he was suspected of being a major arms dealer, as well as a drug baron.

My visit inside Alhaurín was shrouded in secrecy because

the only way I could get in was to pretend to be a friend of Joey's. A few weeks earlier he'd phoned from an illicit jailhouse mobile phone to say he'd been caught up in the police sting and reckoned he'd be in the prison for some months before his lawyer could get the courts to grant him bail. The legal system in Spain works in strange ways. Often a criminal will be arrested, thrown in jail and told he will only be released to await trial if he can provide a certain amount of bail money. As Joey explained: 'That can take months and months and it wears you down. In the end, you cough up the cash – say 20 grand, and you get released and then you fuck off out of there as quickly as possible.'

The Spanish authorities would never admit it, but there seems to be a 'special policy' at work here. If the criminal provides a big enough amount of bail money and then disappears it saves the system hundreds of thousands, maybe even millions of euros in legal expenses and the cost of keeping him in prison. As Joey explained: 'It's a lot cheaper to let me go as long as I leave the country, than to sit there for twenty years soaking up all their cash. It makes sense in a way, doesn't it?'

The guards inside Alhaurín were not particularly forthcoming about their jobs. The ratio of guards to prisoners is 20 to 1, which seems quite good compared with some of the other prisons I have visited across the globe. Incidents of attacks on warders are pretty low, too. But it took the canny public-school educated Joey to explain the significance of that. 'The guards are no different from us, really. Most of them were rejected as policemen. They're badly paid and quite resentful about it so they often sympathise with us, which means some of them are open to bribery.'

Joey had access to a mobile phone 24 hours a day and if that was ever confiscated his cell mate Leon had three more hidden in their quarters. Warders even brought in extra food for inmates if they were prepared to pay for it and there was a special annexed kitchen area near Joey's cell where *cordon bleu* prisoners enjoyed cooking their favourite meals every evening. TV sets were even allowed in the cells.

'It all helps keep things calm here,' explained Joey. 'The guards are alright on the whole. No one seems to mind the backhanders from the inmates to them, although they're not so keen on openly allowing drugs to be brought in.' But Joey then added with a wry smile, 'I've had the best quality cocaine I have ever snorted in my life here in Alhaurín. No one would dare sell bad stuff because we're all in here together and we'd soon find out who cut it.'

Yet despite the supposedly relaxed atmosphere in Alhaurín, it's not always a pleasant place to be in, by any means. 'There are a lot of prisoners here who should be in mental institutions. The Spanish just don't seem to accept that people do have psychological problems and prison is no place for them,' Joey told me.

Before Joey turned up on the Costa del Sol 25 years ago, he was a London-based university-educated professional musician with great hopes of making it as a rock star. Then he got caught up in a £10,000 drug deal and decided to head to the Costa del Crime. 'The guy I bought the drugs from got arrested and I knew it was only a matter of time before the police came after me. I'd heard that Spain was easy to operate in so I booked a flight, packed a bag and turned up here. I've never been back to the UK since.'

Joey quickly settled into the drugs, sex and booze lifestyle that dominates life for so many expats in southern Spain. 'Dealing in big shipments of drugs, puff and coke mainly, was so easy out here back then. The cops were so badly paid they never even chased up cases,' explained Joey. 'They took the attitude that just as long as the criminals were only being horrible to each other then they wouldn't bother with them. In any case, all the cops I've ever met out here all love cocaine. It's their drug of choice and I always made sure that my favourite policemen got as much as they wanted.'

So for the following 20 years Joey built up a drugs empire run through his own gang on the resort of Estepona, just a few kilometres west of Marbella. 'Those were great days,' he continued. 'I had a good crew working for me and I was making half a million a year, spending it all on wine, women and song and even paid for my kids to go to private school. I had a top-of-the-range Mercedes and a house bought for cash. I felt I was untouchable. And you know what? I was in a sense. I dealt drugs like a banker deals in stocks and shares. I was relaxed, confident and never had to get heavy with anyone. My lads did all the direct contact with the punters so I never even had to get my hands dirty. It was a good system out here back in those days.'

Joey soon made strong connections with the Spanish mafia based up in Galicia in north-west Spain, where the majority of cocaine comes in by fishing boats from South America. Joey went on, 'It was really civilised. I'd pop up to Galicia every six weeks or so, organise another shipment, pay over the cash and then get my man to drive it all down here. Then I'd have my team distribute it to all our customers and there was never any aggro.'

Joey reckons that for at least 15 years, the drug trade in this part of southern Spain was 'safer than working as an estate agent'. He explained: 'I looked on myself as a professional businessman. My wife and kids thought that was what I was. The money was rolling in. There was never any violence and I was on top of the world. I felt almost invincible.'

But then Joey got, by his own admission, 'too big for my own fuckin' boots.'

'I bought this club which was basically a brothel and reckoned it would make a nice little sideline and I'd be able to launder all my drugs money through it.'

'Clubs' as they are known in Spain are bars with bedrooms attached, which get around the anti-prostitution laws because the girls who work in the clubs 'rent' the rooms. 'The profit was in the drinks more than the sex,' explained Joey. 'You could charge ten times the normal amount for a beer and the girl had to pay you 25 per cent of her "fee" on top of that.'

But soon after purchasing the club and recruiting girls from as far afield as South America and eastern Europe, Joey was given a stark reminder of what being a criminal on the Costa del Sol was about to become. He told me: 'These two Russians walked into the club and pulled me aside and said they wanted a share of it. I was stunned and told them to fuck off. I couldn't believe they would have the barefaced cheek to think they could lean on me.'

But that incident sparked off a vicious turf war. 'The Russians proved to be complete nutters. They kidnapped my Bulgarian girlfriend and told me they'd slice her ear off if I didn't let them take over control of the club. I was outraged. No one had ever tried to do this to me in all my years in Spain, but times were changing.'

In the end, Joey paid a €100,000 ransom to the Russians and then hired three Romanians to 'teach them a fuckin' lesson.' He explained: 'That whole thing cost me close to a quarter of a million euros. One of the Russians was shot dead and I had to start hiring security staff to protect me and look after the club at all times of the day and night.'

Joey says that 2001 was the year when, 'It all really went fuckin' pear-shaped. The Russians and eastern Europeans had already decided they liked the look of the Costa del Sol as well, and they were turning up here in their droves. It was fuckin' dreadful. I had to start arming myself around the clock and I ended up getting visits from three different gangs trying to get a piece of my club and drugs business off me.'

Joey explained that the foreign gangs were determined to run every single aspect of the criminal scene in southern Spain. 'They were trying to control the girls, the drugs, the people smuggling, the counterfeiting. Everything. But I was caught up in it all and I couldn't just close my operation down and retire to the Balearic Islands. I had mouths to feed and a business to run.'

And there were other problems lurking in the background. The local authorities tried to shut him down because of safety problems with his electricity supply to the club and also said it was a fire hazard. They were out to get him, he said, because he wasn't paying the police enough in bribes at the time.

In order to keep the club open, Joey said he then had to shell out more than € 100,000 in bribes to the local authorities. 'Up until then I'd had nice low outgoings and suddenly in 2001, my outgoings skyrocketed and I was starting to wonder if there would be any profit left for me in the end.'

Then the 9/11 attacks in the US occurred and another, even bigger headache emerged on the horizon, as Joey explained: 'The Government here became obsessed with drugs money being channelled into terrorism and I was getting a lot of pressure put on me by the police for the first time. Until then, you could put quite a few bob in the bank and no one would come after you.

'After all, the black economy out here was running everything until then. I mean, you could buy a house back then and pay cash for it and no one would raise an eyebrow. Then 9/11 happened and suddenly we're all suspected of supporting terrorism. It was really just an excuse to come after us but it hurt us bad.'

Eventually, Joey ended up being nicked by the Spanish police when he delivered a shipment of drugs to the arms trafficker who was under surveillance. 'No one would have taken any notice of that gun dealer in the old days,' he said. 'But the police terrorism unit was on his tail because they reckoned he was supplying terrorists with arms. I walked straight into a trap.'

Joey says he deeply regrets not shutting down his operation many years earlier. 'I knew all this was coming but like so many others I thought I was untouchable. I really believed that all these foreigners would shoot each other down and then it would just go back to the way it was all those years earlier.'

Joey even acknowledges that he is 'one of the lucky ones'.

'Being arrested was a blessing in disguise in a sense,' he admits, 'because I'm sure I would have got gunned down by one of those psycho foreigners in the end.'

The worldwide recession will, Joey predicts, cause even more problems on the Costa del Sol. He believes too many properties have been built for the holiday market and prices have crashed, so none of the villains are putting their money into property any more. 'In the end, the demand for coke and other drugs will drop and that's when all the crims will get really desperate and come out shooting. It's going to get even more deadly on the Costa del Sol. I've heard of people being shot over a € 500 debt. It's got out of hand but I can only see it getting worse.'

A few weeks after our interview, Joey slipped out of Spain

following his release on bail from Alhaurín. He then admitted in a call to me that he wouldn't ever be back on the Costa del Sol. He was heading for South America. 'This place is finished. It's on the scrapheap and it's about to implode. I reckon it's going to get even more deadly out here. I'm going to scrape a living together somehow but drugs are now a thing of the past for me. I lost my club, my house, and everything after I was arrested and now I have a chance to make a clean start a long way from all the madness.'

2

DOWN ON THE south coast of Spain, the smells and fear that dominate Alhaurín jail are never far from the minds of the hyped-up, overactive coke-addicted gangsters scraping a living in places like Fuengirola – a poor man's version of Marbella, which is sandwiched between the more glamorous bits of this coastline and Málaga Airport. Fuengirola is a five-mile strip of grey sand and concrete and must be the only place on earth where you can meet more people called 'Lee' outside of prison than inside. An incredible 40 per cent of all cars stolen in Europe are nicked on the Costa del Sol.

At one large Fuengirola supermarket just off the main N340 coast route known to many as the 'road of death' because of the large number of car crashes that occur on it, many British hoods sit and sip a coffee and a brandy while negotiating the purchase of guns and drugs. The first time I walked into this den of crime, I noticed every single voice in the canteen was English and male. Some were even waiting for their girlfriends and wives to do the weekly shop while they sat wheeler-dealing with other criminals.

I was introduced to this, the most notorious gangland café on the entire coastline, by a young villain called Mark, who promised me I could buy any gun, a brand new passport, or a UK driving licence through the shady Arthur Daley-style characters who have turned this place into a sunshine version of the fictional Winchester Club, which featured in the hit TV show *Minder*.

When I met Mark in the car park outside the supermarket he warned me, 'No one will deal with you as a first-time customer, but once they get used to you being there, they might start offering up stuff.' In fact it took two more visits to the café before I actually sat down and started negotiations with a Scottish man in his thirties called Gerry. 'I can get you shooters, passports, UK driving licences all for a price,' he said. 'What are you after?' I later discovered that this was the very same place where notorious gangster Kenneth Noye came when he was on the run from British police following the road-rage death of a young motorist on the M25 more than ten years before.

Gerry explained: 'Shooters take a week to deliver but it depends what you're after. The passports and the driving licences take much longer.' I told Gerry I was after a revolver. 'One thousand euros. Seven-fifty up front. The rest on delivery.' I said I'd get back to him.

My visit to that supermarket café seemed to confirm what so many criminals had been telling me – that the Costa del Sol's underworld was still thriving right under the noses of the police and hundreds of thousands of tourists. I never did follow up on my request but I bumped into Gerry a few weeks later in a notorious villain's bar on the front at Fuengirola. When I apologised for not getting back to him he said coolly, 'Don't worry about it, pal. I had an order for ten shooters the next day so it went right out of my mind.'

My original Fuengirola contact, Mark, told me that he'd been in southern Spain for three years and had initially been shocked at the state of the underworld out here. 'There's such a crazy mix of different nationalities and they're all chasing the same stuff: drugs and hookers. I came out here with a couple of mates planning to run a bit of puff (cannabis) but the prices have dipped so badly that I've had to get into other stuff.'

That 'other stuff' includes cigarettes and people-smuggling back to the UK. 'The key is the contacts you have back in Britain. If you've got them you can set up all sorts of things out here. But you have to keep it all really low-key because if the eastern Europeans or South Americans get wind of what you're up to they always try to get a slice of it.'

Mark, who comes from Gloucester originally, says he has resisted the temptation to be armed at all times but says he always carries a knife under the front seat of his car 'just in case'. He explained: 'I run a team of three, which is sensible. Keep it small and then the nutters stay away from you. But once you start expanding, someone will always come after you.'

At one stage, Mark got into illegal gambling from certain bars on the seafront at Fuengirola. 'There's a lot of very bored people out here with a few bob that they've saved up over the years and they like gambling, so these illegal bookmakers have set up shop in a few bars out here.'

Mark's 'work' involves chasing up debts incurred by some of these illegal gamblers. 'It's easy money because you never go through with any threats. The other day me and the lads had to pay this businessman a visit at his villa in Calahonda because he owed a bookie ten grand from six months back. Well I can tell you that within an hour of us turning up at his house, this fella had paid up. We didn't need to do anything violent. We just told him we'd been sent to get his debt repaid and he got the message loud and clear.'

But Mark says that in recent years there has been an unhealthy 'crossover' between the British gangsters and the foreign contingent. 'It's fuckin' scary at times. I'm here minding my own business and these bastards just come in waving guns and expecting to get a chunk of what we're doing. Its completely out of order.'

Mark revealed that many of the eastern European gangsters are settling in Spain *after* spending time in the UK. 'It's outrageous. A lot of them take their families to Britain, get settled in, claim all the relevant benefits and then dump their families on the state in the UK and head over here to find themselves new opportunities. The trouble is that makes them even more dangerous because they know how the Brit crims operate. They know that we hardly ever use real violence and so they think they can intimidate us.'

Mark says that a couple of months ago he met a Russian hooker in a bar and ended up going to a hotel with her. 'Then halfway through doing the business this Romanian pair burst into the room and demanded my wallet and all my cash. It had all been a scam and if I ever see those two bastards again I know who I am going to phone to have them permanently taken care of.'

But Mark admits that this sort of violent response is the basis of so many problems on the Costa del Sol. 'It's all about hitting out first before you're crushed by the opposition. I don't like resorting to violence but I don't know what else to do. It's a bit of a nightmare scenario because more and more people are going to get topped as a result.'

Mark says Fuengirola is a lot more dangerous than anywhere back in Britain. 'This place is so dodgy. If you upset the wrong person you can end up in a wooden box. I've started avoiding certain bars now because there are so many coke-fuelled nutters waiting for any chance to have a pop at you. It's fucking frightening.'

But Mark and many other younger British gangsters are literally trapped in Spain to a certain degree. 'Look. It's much easier to be a crim out here because the police still don't seem to give a fuck but the recession is biting hard and its got harder and harder to make decent money. The trouble is that it would be even more expensive to move back to Britain. It's a no-win situation. I'm hoping I can ride it out here because having the sea and the sunshine is a lot more pleasant than anything on offer back home.'

So who exactly are these 'nutty' foreign criminals who are taking on the Brits at their own game? In the middle of researching this book I met a Romanian gangster called Sly who seemed to prove the very point Mark was making. Sly, 32, had married a British woman called Val – who was 30 years his senior – three years earlier. Ironically, that helped him to stay in Spain, although Romania's recent acceptance into the EU has made that irrelevant these days.

Sly provided a chilling insight into the gang wars on the Costas. I was astounded when he began telling me the inner secrets of his gang and how it was all perfectly normal in the world where he came from. 'In Romania life is cheap,' said Sly in a very relaxed manner. 'Spain is like paradise compared with my home country.'

Sly didn't take much persuading to open up. He looked and acted extremely hard and his piercing blue eyes seemed to be boring holes into my conscience. Yet in the middle of telling me some of the most horrific things, Sly would suddenly start giggling and nudge his wife Val and then kiss her full on the lips almost as if he was seeking her approval for everything, even the most evil acts of criminality he was describing. Sly would have stabbed me in the back as soon as look at me if I crossed him. I had no doubt of that, but there was this strange childlike side to him. I later found out he had spent much of his childhood in an orphanage. Maybe that's where it all came from.

Sly told me in calm, clinical terms what he did to his enemies if they ever fought back. 'I slit their throat like this,' he said, smiling as he did the traditional finger movement across my neck. It was truly chilling.

Sly said that he often stalked his prey if he had vengeance

on his mind. 'Listen. I like the English. I am married to an English lady but they are too old-fashioned. They don't really want to hurt people and we know that, so we take over their businesses. It's easy.'

Sly said he regularly tortured other gangsters who threatened him. 'Sometimes you have no choice. Last month I had a problem with this Bulgarian who was trying to set up a rival business on my territory. As soon as I heard what was happening, three of us went to find him. We took him to the mountains and left him out in the sun to dry.'

I didn't dare ask exactly what he meant by that but it sounded pretty obvious. But that wasn't all. Sly continued: 'We had trouble with the Chinese a while back. They are crazy motherfuckers and we knew we would have to kill one of them to send out a message so we kidnapped three of them from a brothel and took them to an apartment. The Chinese are so weird. None of them seemed scared, even when I started burning one guy's eyelids. So I got my man Igor to cut him up a bit. Then we left him to bleed by the side of the *carretera* (road). It's a message to the other Chinese to stay out of our affairs. I think it must be working because they have been very quiet recently.'

Just then Sly put his hand into his jacket pocket. I hesitated for a minute, dreading what he might be about to pull out. It was a tiny cosh. He handed it to me. 'Feel that. It is steel. I can break a man's jaw with one hit.'

He was right. This small three-inch weapon weighed a lot and yet it was no bigger than my middle finger. Sly took the cosh back from me and sat there stroking it in an almost obscene fashion. 'This is my little baby. He does lots of things for me.'

Just then Sly demonstrated his love for his little 'baby' by thwacking the weapon into his palm in a series of flat, vicious blows. 'See? It is most effective and yet when I pull it out people think it's nothing. It is good to surprise them.'

Aiming for the face it not only hurts but could also cause the maximum damage. Sly said he'd lash out at anyone who got in his way. 'I had to use it on this Russian woman because she wouldn't give me the phone number of another criminal I wanted to find,' explained Sly. 'The Russians are the worst. They don't give a fuck and the women are even harder than the men. This bitch just looked at me like I was some piece of shit when I asked her nicely so I used this on her until she co-operated. And you know what? Afterwards she still spat in my face.' Sly laughed then, almost as if the woman's defiance had impressed him, despite his contempt for her.

Sly told me the same treatment was handed out to anyone – man, woman or child – who crossed him and his gang or even breached gang rules, especially the code of silence. It was clear that if people like Sly came after you, they'd stab you or shoot you for real. The scars and laceration marks on Sly's own face and body were evidence of that.

Sly said that even if an enemy survived a beating or a stabbing, he could expect Sly and his men to come after him again. 'We don't want people thinking we are soft in the head. It's important that your enemies know you will still come back to punish them further. That fear often stops them defying you any more.'

Sly himself confessed that back in Romania he himself had had to pass certain tests in order to become a member of a local criminal gang. 'I was expected to stab a policeman in our town. The boss at the time chose the policeman they wanted to be hurt. I was given his name and the police station where he worked and then I went and found him.'

Sly refused to say what happened to that first victim but he did explain how that first attack had evolved. 'I knew that it was a condition of my membership. When I asked them how I would hurt this policeman they just told me that a knife would be given to me and I would then have to go and find him and hurt him badly.'

Although Sly had already refused to go into any details of that first attack, I decided to press him further and asked him what happened.

Sly hesitated for a few moments and I started to wonder if he was getting angry that I'd ignored his earlier pledge not to discuss the incident. But then he took a deep breath, leaned down closer to me and started talking once more. 'I was walking to the shop near my home and this man came up to me in the middle of the street and handed me a plastic bag. In it was the knife. That was when I knew they were being serious and I would have to go through with the attack if I wanted to join the gang.'

There was another pause as Sly collected his thoughts, then he continued. 'I found the policeman walking out of the police station and followed him for about five minutes until he was walking down an unlit street. I stabbed him in the back three times and then left him on the ground. I know he survived but he never worked as a policeman again and I discovered later that he had molested a little girl so maybe that was part of the reason why I was asked to attack him.'

Considering the strict code of silence that exists, particularly between eastern European gangs, I was surprised at how open Sly had been. But I wanted to know more about his life and crimes in Spain because that was key to my book and revealing the real extent of the underworld out here in the Mediterranean sunshine.

Sly was a bizarre mix. He was tall, with jet-black wavy hair and startlingly pale blue eyes, and there was an almost effeminate air to him. Yet there was definitely a lot of macho stuff going on when it came to these kinds of eastern European gangs. After all, men like Sly had to prove their courage and suffer in silence at all times. There were clearly so many dark secrets inside Sly's head.

So I turned to Sly's British wife Val and pressed her in the hope she might be more open about the Romanians on the Costa del Sol. What she told me was terrifying. Val said that Sly had been the victim of a vicious rape as a 12-year-old in the orphanage where he was brought up and 'that turned him into a mean and nasty person'. Val insisted that despite this, Sly had many redeeming characteristics and that was why she'd married him, convinced she could change him into a normal human being. I had my doubts.

Val said that after that appalling abuse, Sly 'grew up very fast' and ran away from the orphanage and ended up living with a gang of kids in the slums of Bucharest. He even become one of the notorious 'tunnel children' who still live to this day in the sewers of the city.

'Sly never had a chance,' explained Val. 'That doesn't mean he should be forgiven for all the bad things he's done but it does tell you why he's ended up being the person he is.'

Val said that Sly and a group of other kids formed a gang, which still exists in part on the Costa del Sol. 'Sly and his friends trust no one other than each other. That's how they have survived. He and two others came out here a couple of years ago because he kept being arrested and put in prison and he had had enough. The trouble is that Sly only knows one way to make money and that's by committing crimes.'

Back in Romania the tunnel kids gang – featuring Sly and his friends – soon gained a notorious reputation within Bucharest's criminal fraternity. Sly and his comrades were literally living underground in a series of open sewers under the city. They specialised in brutal hit-and-run type crimes on local businesses and people. By the time the over-stretched police came on the scene, the gang would have long since disappeared back beneath the surface of the city.

Sly and his gang specialised in robbing people who were often defenceless, and they soon had a chilling reputation in Bucharest. They terrorised the warren of tunnels beneath the surface of the streets, making sure that no strangers invaded their 'space'. Legends and myths grew about Sly and his gang, according to Val. Even after they'd grown up they continued living in the tunnels, and there was talk about them having wives and children.

It was only when there was a government-inspired cleanup ordered by authorities that Sly and his gang members realised they needed to flee from Romania. Spain seemed the perfect destination.

Val admitted that no one knew all the gang's secrets but at least by giving me some of the background to Sly's development as a criminal, I could start to get a handle on why he was so cold-blooded. 'There is a good person in there, I'm sure,' said Val. 'I'm going to help him escape this life and I know we are going to end up having a better life together than he could possibly ever have had on his own.'

Val's words sounded a tad green, but I was the last person to feel I had the right to shoot her down in flames on that one. I was learning about how characters like Sly ended up creating havoc in places like Spain. 'It's so much easier for me to operate out here,' interrupted Sly who had reappeared halfway through my conversation with Val and now wanted to take over the interview once again.

But, I asked, could you ever leave the gang as Val hopes you will? 'Look,' he replied. 'The gang is my life. I would not have anything if it were not for the gang.' Val looked crestfallen at that last remark but Sly seemed determined not to give her the wrong impression, which was admirable in its own way.

'There is no way out of the gang, except by dying,' explained Sly in a very matter-of-fact voice. 'I cannot survive without them.' Sly said it was his idea to bring the gang over to Spain. 'I recognised that it was a safer place for us, rather than, say, London.'

'Safer?' I asked.

'Yes, the Spanish don't really care what we do as long as it does not involve their citizens.' The one secret Sly refused to reveal was the name of his gang. 'That's between us only. That way if we have any impostors we find out very quickly and dispose of them.'

3

OBVIOUSLY NOT ALL the gangs on the Costa del Sol are run on such rigid rules. Down the coast from seedy Fuengirola lies Puerto Banus, a 'blingy' offshoot to Marbella and home to more gold-encrusted villains than probably anywhere else on earth. It has a marina with dozens of ten-million-pound-plus yachts tied up, and more Ferraris than anywhere outside Italy.

Overlooking the water's edge are dozens of bars and restaurants, including a select few where most of Britain's old-style gangsters still hang out to this day. Bernie is one of the most familiar old 'faces' on the Costa del Sol and he told me that today's up-and-coming young hoods are in danger of turning this infamous strip of coastline into an underworld no-go area.

'It's all got completely fuckin' out of hand in recent years,' explained Bernie, sucking on a king-size cigar and a vodka and tonic. 'The youngsters who are coming through the ranks now are complete and utter psychos. It's bedlam out there and a lot of innocent people are being knocked off for no good reason.'

Bernie, now in his late sixties, is still looked on by the younger British criminals as one of the few 'real' British villains in southern Spain. 'I get a lot of respect out here because I've got form,' explained Bernie. And by 'form' he means he's been in prison for killing a criminal rival and also took part in one of London's most notorious bank robberies more than a quarter of a century ago.

Bernie admits that he still 'works' from time to time and boasts that he's free to move around the coast without fear of retribution from rival gangsters. 'In fact some of the so-called new boys come to me for advice,' said Bernie between puffs on his fat cigar.

'I've been here for more than 20 years and when I saw some of these foreign crims turning up here a few years back, I told my mates in the 'business' to watch out because some of these characters are fuckin' nutters.' Bernie claims he's even carefully nurtured some of the biggest new names on the Costa del Sol.

'I went in to see them all and told them what I liked to do out here and how I didn't expect any of them to interfere with my operations. It's funny because all the other Brits out here said I was barking mad but I reckon it's paid off handsomely. I really do.'

When I met Bernie at his favourite watering hole overlooking the yachts and sports cars in the marina at Puerto Banus, he claimed he'd just come from a meeting with a man who represented one of the richest oligarchs in Russia. 'He's on the make like all the rest of them,' explained Bernie, who was wearing the obligatory white trousers and white shoes that were all the rage back in the opulent eighties. Bernie had met the Russian billionaire at the swish

Marbella Club, just up the road from Puerto Banus and a renowned location for passing rock stars and royalty.

Besides the thick-set gold necklace around his neck, Bernie also had a Bobby Charlton-style sweep of the remainder of his suspiciously chestnut-tinted hair across his bald pate. In some ways he looked like an extra from the hit TV show *Life On Mars*. The bar we were talking in was decked out in garish swirled wallpaper and looked as if it hadn't had a lick of paint since Bernie had bought himself those flashy white winkle-pickers during the reign of Margaret Thatcher.

As we were talking, a beautiful brunette Latino woman in tight jeans glanced across at Bernie and smiled. He winked back and then continued with his overview of the gang wars raging on the Costa del Sol. 'It's changing out here all the time. A lot of the older Brits have moved to Thailand and Costa Rica and places like that because it's too fuckin' crowded here these days.'

But how come, if that was the case, Bernie hung on here? 'I'm above all these shoot-ups and shit like that. I've been bedded down here for so long I wouldn't know how to survive anywhere else.' And survival is the key word here. For Bernie seemed to have an ability to duck and dive his way out of trouble.

He recalled: 'About a year ago this bunch of Poles turned up in the port (Puerto Banus) and started giving it large in all directions. They bought themselves a flash yacht, a couple of Mercedes and a load of hookers and gave the impression they were made men. Well, if there's one thing the Russians don't like it's a Pole. When they heard about this gang they made it their business to run them out of town. It was a right bloody massacre in the end. The Russians employ these fruitcake Latvian ex-paratroopers as bodyguards and for general security and they abseiled on to the yacht one night, sprayed it with bullets and then left a couple of firebombs behind for good measure. The Poles got the message and were never seen again.'

Bernie makes light of it all but there is a serious point to what he is saying. 'I take the attitude that I can sit back and let them all wipe each other out. Then once the dust has settled I'll stroll back into the limelight.' Bernie says his main priority is to make sure his face doesn't end up looking like he's been through a car crash.

Saturday night in Puerto Banus still brings out all the remaining British gangsters. Many of them watch the footie on the telly in a couple of select bars. Then, as evening draws in, they pull out their sachets of cocaine and start getting hyped up. As darkness falls and the chemicals kick in, many of the gang bosses flex their muscles a bit and look around to see who's watching them. The atmosphere is akin to a scene from *Goodfellas*, with coked-up little characters who look a bit like Joe Pesci marching up and down to the gents to replenish their hits of white powder.

Sergi is a Ukrainian 'businessman' who has lived on the Costa del Sol for three years. I was introduced to him by one of the British old-timers one Saturday night in a badly lit bar in Puerto Banus. 'The trouble with you British is that you drink too much and you take too much cocaine,' said Sergi. His British mate sitting next to him laughed so loudly it sounded completely false. 'Where I come from we can hold our drink and we don't take drugs because then we are not in control.'

I soon found out why Sergi was the only non-British man in the bar that night. It turned out that he employed more than 20 Brits for his 'businesses.' I was intrigued as to why he did that. 'Oh I like the British way of life. The loyalty. The humour. I don't trust my countrymen, especially when they are out here. They would kill you as soon as look at you if you had something they wanted.'

Sergi then went on to provide a fascinating insight into the criminal hierarchy on the Costa del Sol and why the gang wars could eventually implode this whole area. 'It's just too easy here to run businesses like mine.' I stopped him there and asked what his 'businesses' were? Sergi smiled and looked me straight in the eye. 'They are very profitable. That is all you need to know.'

He continued: 'Sometimes I have to make an example of my enemies. I don't like doing it but in the long term it helps stop a lot of what I will call "unfortunate incidents".' Sergi refused to be drawn on exactly what action he had taken but suffice to say it must have resulted in someone being physically harmed.

Surely, I asked, the police are a problem? 'It's like my country in that respect,' said Sergi. 'The police can be bought. They are badly paid and grateful for anything I can offer them.' Sergi claims that one policeman even asked if he could work for him part-time while continuing to serve in Marbella's Policía Nacional. 'I wasn't surprised. He'd just got divorced and needed to earn more money in order to pay off his ex-wife. We all have these problems.'

Sergi said the local police tolerate the activities of the gangs on the Costa del Sol because there is little else they can do. 'They don't have the manpower or the resources to investigate every single crime,' explained Sergi. 'It's almost as if they are happy for us to continue bringing money into the economy because it means a better life for everyone down here. They need us here. It's been like this for so long the whole place would collapse if criminals were not operating here.' Sergi was very careful not to include himself when he used the word 'criminals'.

Most gangs down here on the Costa del Sol are involved in drugs, prostitution, robbery and fraud. Yet Sergi had a fair point. The more successful the criminal and the more people he or she employed, the more money generated for the local economy. It's the biggest irony of life in southern Spain.

As it became increasingly clear when I met these gangsters that I was trying to present a warts-and-all look at the underworld in Spain, I was granted an audience with one of the most feared British gangsters of all time, who had resided in the Costa del Sol for three years.

We'll call him 'Stan' because even if I used only his real Christian name, every other criminal would know precisely who I was talking about. 'Stan' is a member of one of the UK's most famous criminal families. He had heard about my efforts to write this book and wanted to 'get a few things straight'.

Stan might have been in his mid-sixties but he stood ramrod straight and spoke with a soft voice that seemed to underline his hardness in a twisted way. He wasn't massive by any means but he had the darkest eyes I have ever encountered. They were matt black cesspools with not a flicker of emotion in them.

Stan knew all the players on the Costa del Crime and I suspected he was still operating with impunity along the entire coastline. Yet he seemed very relaxed as we spoke in a Spanish restaurant situated far away from the usual criminal haunts. Earlier he'd rolled into the car park driving a brand new Spanish-registered Range Rover.

'I don't like those hooker joints full of coked-up villains,' Stan told me. 'I appreciate Spain for what it really is: a wonderful, diverse place full of easy-going pleasant people who enjoy a rich, good lifestyle compared to all the miserable sods back in Blighty.'

With Stan I felt I was in the company of someone very menacing, but he had this ability to make it all sound so normal. 'Look. I ain't no angel but I've run a very successful group of businesses down the years and a lot of people have got very rich off the back of me.'

Leaning forward, Stan clocked me long and hard for a few moments and then just like the managing director of crime that he was, he tried to put me at my ease. 'Listen. I know where I come from. I know that certain things have had to be done to ensure my businesses are kept afloat but we are in troubled times now and we all need to be more sensible.'

It dawned on me that Stan was hoping to use me to send out a message to his criminal rivals to stay calm and avoid the very gang wars this book is highlighting. I couldn't help feeling it was all a little bit late for that. Stan must have guessed my intentions because he went on, 'I know you're going to write about all the killings and the mischief and the drugs and all that stuff. There's no denying this place is a cesspit in that respect but we have to survive don't we?'

I wasn't sure how to respond to that one. After all, what rights did a multimillionaire hood whose fortune was based on illegal drugs have to survive? But I didn't take Stan up on that point. Instead I asked him about the current situation and who was likely to suffer the most.

'It's the Brits who are taking the most knocks. No doubt about it. A lot of these characters are getting on now and we all come from a time when business was business but you never overlapped into people's normal lives. We considered ourselves soldiers.

'If one of us got killed because of a deal that went pear-shaped, then that was the way it was. It's the risk we've all taken down the years. Sure it's sad when anyone dies but if you are a soldier then you have to deal with that sort of stuff. But today it's different – the up-and-coming youngsters are causing chaos and we're all suffering as a result.'

Stan cited a classic example a couple of years ago when an

Irish criminal and his family were targeted by a hit squad after a drugs deal went wrong. 'That was fucking outrageous,' said Stan. 'I heard this bloke was in trouble with a mob of eastern Europeans and they went after him, but to target his wife and kids as well. That's out of order. What is the world coming to when that sort of thing happens?'

Stan admitted that back in Britain, foreign gangs have not made such a terrifying impression on the home-grown criminals. 'I hate to say it but the coppers are smarter back in the UK and that's made it harder for these foreign bastards to get a toehold. The cops out here are fucking useless. It's worked to our advantage for years but now we're paying the price for it.' And none of this was said with even a hint of irony.

Stan told me all about what he calls 'the real fuckin' underworld' that exists on the Costa del Sol. 'I came here a few years back because I knew I could run everything from here with a lot less hassle. At first it was fine. Some of the foreigners popped up now and again but I made sure they realised I was running my own outfit and by and large they left me alone.'

But, says Stan, a new desperation has crept into the criminal atmosphere these days. 'The middle-of-the-road fellas are making fuck-all money now. Before, they could make a quick drugs deal, buy a house for cash and turn it around for a healthy profit and no one was the wiser. But the recession kicked off here way before it hit the UK and that's changed all the rules.'

'What do you mean by the rules?' I asked.

Stan narrowed his eyes. 'They've got too fuckin' desperate and they're running around in circles. That's why there's so much bloodshed out here these days. There's no money for anything any more and no one wants to share the profits, either. Do you know, the other day one of my oldest mates out here was almost topped just because some Bulgarian fucker decided he wouldn't share the profits from a deal even though they'd been doing that sort of business together for years.'

Stan continued: 'It's like a great big spider's web out here and if you get caught up in it there is no escape. I've still got most people's respect out here because my reputation is well known but I stay out of the web deliberately. That's why I'm meeting you here in an ordinary Spanish restaurant off the beaten track. Those mugs down in the port are asking for trouble. They're rubbing people's noses in it and that's when the trouble starts.'

'But,' I pressed, 'who is running things out here these days?' Stan took one of his customary deep breaths and continued: 'You just wouldn't believe some of the characters pulling strings out here these days. There are two fellas whose names appear in the papers all the time as billionaires and they're probably cleaning up two thirds of all the "business" out here. It's bloody outrageous but there's no point taking them on because they are more powerful than anyone you've ever come across.'

Stan then proceeded to name these two 'kingpins' and I was

stunned because they are both supposedly responsible law-abiding businessmen back in their home country. 'These blokes have got whole governments in their pockets. When the Spanish elected a new left-wing government a couple of years back, I presumed these two characters would quieten down a bit. Far from it. They just chucked some huge bucks in the direction of a few officials in the new government and next thing you know they're back to running things down here.'

Stan admits he keeps a low profile here on the Costa del Sol these days but that doesn't mean he is no longer a very powerful force to be reckoned with. 'They know who I am and I know who they are. Let's just leave it at that shall we?' I didn't argue.

Speaking with the kind of chilling focus that could halt a Chieftain tank on a battlefield, Stan went on to tell me his fears for the future of the Costa del Sol. His face creased up with seriousness as he went on: 'The bloodbath is going to get worse. These trigger-happy youngsters don't seem to have a fear of death like we did. It's all live for today because we might be gone by tomorrow stuff. But it's stupid and short-sighted because the harder it is to operate, the less produce gets out there, which means demand falls and in the end it'll all collapse.'

The scariest thing about Stan was not his menacing smile or his shark-dead eyes. No, it was the way he sounded so in control of his emotions. It was as if he was saying he had already stepped back from the bedlam and was going to watch all the rest of the underworld obliterate itself.

Meanwhile, on the Costa del Sol the restaurants and bars and clubs that used to be thriving are all empty most of the time or closed down permanently. I kept noticing how much deader the atmosphere was than even just a few years back when everyone seemed to be soaking up the sunshine of a never-ending economic boom.

Stan reckoned he had seen it all before and issued the following stark warning: 'Crime thrives during recessions but the trouble is that there are all these desperate characters out there with no money and no idea how to work properly. They're going to start nicking the 'work' off other smaller operators and then World War Three will break out. God help us.

'They're all living in these gated communities in order to stop others from robbing them but they're the ones being robbed blind by the banks and mortgage brokers. The perfect life they thought they could find here no longer exists.'

4

SO, THE GANG war on the Costa del Sol is deadly and vastly complex. I needed to visit the other areas of it where many, much less wealthy Brits have settled over the last 20 years. Take Benalmadena, to the east of Fuengirola. It's a badly policed area filled with mainly working-class Brits, many of whom are claiming unemployment benefit through relatives back in the more deprived areas of Britain.

The centre of Benalmadena is dominated by scruffy tower blocks and it's clear from the people out on the streets that this is a much more down-market location. Everyone on the Costa del Sol knows all about Benalmadena. Gangs in Benalmadena tend to consist of much younger criminals and it's estimated that there are at least a dozen gangs operating in the vicinity. A lot of their time is spent fighting one another for control of turf. Frankie has just turned 20 and hails from Newcastle originally, but his parents moved back to the north-east of England three years ago and he's been ducking and diving ever since.

'I love it out here but it's hard at the moment,' said Frankie. He agreed to talk to me after his family had helped me with another TV crime project a few years ago. But, I asked Frankie, how was he surviving? 'I run a little team, I s'pose you could call them a gang but that sounds like clowns. But we're professional criminals and we make a good living. Simple as that.'

Drugs are obviously the backbone of Frankie's operation. His turf includes the notorious '24-hour square', a haven of ugly bars and alleyways that backs on to a McDonald's restaurant. Hundreds, and in the summer season thousands, of disaffected British youths meet on Friday and Saturday nights here and the police are constantly breaking up brawls; knife fights are virtually two a penny. 'In 24-hour square we can make ten grand a night at weekends in the winter and that doubles in the holiday season,' said Frankie.

But with those sorts of profits – from the sale of cocaine, MDMA powder, ecstasy and cannabis – come high risks. Frankie says he runs the only totally British gang in Benalmadena. 'Most of the other Brits did a runner because the foreigners scared the shit out of them,' he explained.

Hard drugs like coke and MDMA are easier to shift because they are sold in such small packets and they yield a much higher profit. But those particular narcotics have sparked lots of problems. Outside gangs regularly try and take over Frankie's turf and in the past year alone he says there have been three near-fatal incidents. 'You have to show them you can't be pushed around or else they keep coming back. I carry a blade on me the whole time but sometimes when it gets hairy out there I have to pack a shooter. I tend to flash it at people just to make sure they know how serious I am and that usually does the trick.'

Two separate gangs of Albanian gangsters had been trying to muscle in on 24-hour square in recent months and Frankie knows only too well that they will be back. 'They're fuckin' mad those Albanians. Last time they turned up and tried flogging coke right out in the open on my fuckin' territory. So I went and got three of my boys and we moved straight in on those Albanian fuckers. They were all armed but we caught them out in the open so they didn't pull out their weapons. I suppose we were lucky in a way.'

Frankie refused to explain what actually happened to his Albanian rivals but it's clear that he believes others will be back to try and scare him off. 'The Brits have a bad reputation for bottling out of things round here and I have to keep doing certain things to make sure they all know I mean business.'

Frankie claims that there are so many local jobless Brits that a few of them have even offered him money to be allowed to join his gang. 'These kids want to belong,' explained Frankie. 'Most of them are just like me. Their mum and dad have fucked off back to Britain and they've stayed because it's the only home they know and they are prepared to do anything to survive. It's not a good situation but it means there's no shortage of recruits for me.'

But Frankie, a wise head on such young shoulders, predicts that more problems will occur when some of these disaffected young Brits decide to set up gangs of their own. 'It's going to happen for sure. Nobody's got any cash out here so they've gotta start thieving. The war is going to get even nastier when that happens.'

Frankie admits that in order to survive as a gangster on the Costa del Sol, the younger British criminals are having to adopt an 'if you can't beat 'em join 'em' attitude. 'That means everyone's going to have to be tooled up to protect their turf. It's dog eat dog out there.'

Before Frankie and his contemporaries came onto the scene, most of the narcotics business in Benalmadena and neighbouring Torremolinos was run by big-time drug barons who controlled the entire coastline between Málaga and Estepona. But all that started to fragment about five years ago because of the influx of eastern Europeans. 'When I was a kid at school here, the coke and puff was supplied by street dealers who were answerable to proper, serious criminal faces but all that's changed. It's easy now to find a major supplier, organise your own transportation and run an operation off your own back. The biggest challenge is the territory. I had to pay good money for my turf at the square and no one is going to bully me off it.'

So with young high-flyers on the horizon, it promises to get a lot more violent on the streets of Benalmadena. To all the aspiring, disaffected youngsters roaming the streets of this run-down resort, people like Frankie are heroes to be looked up to. But, typically, Frankie knows that sort of hero worship won't last long.

'One day these same kids will be after what's mine and that's when the shooting begins,' explained Frankie, who walks with a limp after one rival gang member ran over his shin during a fight about drug dealing. Frankie refused to talk about the incident except to say, 'I couldn't let that one go. The bloke who did this to me is not around any more.' He refused to say whether that meant his rival was dead or had simply left Spain.

Frankie still lives in the same run-down apartment his parents abandoned three years earlier. He says the landlord still thinks his parents are living there. 'I've kept up the rental payments and it suits me fine here. It's nothing flash, which is always better when you're in this game. The people who give it large all over the place are the ones who either end up in the mountains or down the local nick.'

Frankie shares the flat with his 16-year-old girlfriend Donna, who comes from Darlington. Her parents went back to the UK a year ago and she has brought herself up alone ever since. Frankie has some strong views on the way they were both abandoned, which shows that he's a lot more reflective than one might think at first. 'I'm doing what I'm doing because they basically dumped me here. It's not a nice thing to do and Donna's mum did it to her when she was even younger. No wonder I've had to resort to crime, eh?'

The living room in Frankie's flat is bare apart from the obligatory widescreen TV, which cost him a whopping two grand. 'It's me only real luxury. I even drive around in a Ford Fiesta so people don't think I'm up to no good.'

But Frankie did admit that he's putting all his money away so that one day he can go straight and live a 'normal' life. 'I don't want to do this forever. I just want enough cash to be able to buy myself a nice house and settle down with Donna and have kids. I'll set up a company – a straight company – and try and make somethin' of my life. You know I knew this drug dealer fella when I was 15 and he told me that you never spend longer than five years in this business because if you do, you'll get nicked or killed in the end.'

Meanwhile, Frankie admitted he was fighting other demons in the shape of a clear and obvious addiction to cocaine. 'I love the fuckin' stuff and that's my weakness because all the cleverest people in this business don't take the produce. I was the same until about a year ago and then a mate of mine persuaded me to have a line and now I can't get enough of it. I'm fuckin' hooked and I hate myself for it in a way but on the other hand it does help get me through the days and nights.'

Moments later, Frankie pulled out a sachet and expertly chopped himself out a line of cocaine. It was interesting to note that his girlfriend Donna did not partake. Frankie later told me, 'I'd never go out with a bird who was hooked on this shit. It's the devil's fuckin' candy.'

By the time I finally got out of Frankie's tatty apartment, I felt deadened by the sight of a young man on the edge of either dying from drug addiction or being gunned down in a fight about a drug dealer's turf. It struck me that he couldn't win either way. But how different his life might have turned out if his parents had not simply abandoned him when they left Benalmadena and headed back to the UK.

But in the middle of all this gang-related crime, there were the good guys trying their hardest to clean up the crime-riddled streets. Ex-drug dealer Walter was a classic example. Now in his sixties, he had run with a gang of dope peddlers in the 1980s in Torremolinos and almost died during an argument with a gang rival. Now cleaned up and working for the local drug rehabilitation centre, Walter has earned the respect of many on the Costa del Crime because he never takes sides. One gang member had told me to talk to Walter because he knew both sides of the coin – literally.

Walter's own girlfriend died of a heroin overdose when they lived together in his native Bristol. He'd first come out to Spain to escape the pain and heartbreak of losing her but then got caught up with the 'wrong crowd', and even ended up spending a year in Málaga's notorious Alhaurín prison.

On his release, Walter was approached by a gang in Torremolinos to be one of their street dealers. 'Men of my age were in great demand back then because we didn't look as obvious as the young dealers,' explained Walter. But then an incident happened which changed the course of Walter's life.

'It was my first night as a street dealer and this young girl came up to me and tried to score some heroin off me,' he explained. 'I was horrified. I mean I only sold coke and puff, but seeing that girl reminded me of what had happened to my girlfriend back in Bristol and I felt so ashamed that I had allowed myself to be sucked back into it all. I quit on the spot and decided to turn all my experience into something positive.'

Now Walter spends much of his time patrolling the streets of Torremolinos seeking out drug addicts and gangsters alike and trying to talk to them about their lives in the hope they might reconsider the paths they have taken. 'I work in a shop in the day and then try to get out most nights. I know all the areas where the drugs are sold openly. It's the same places as when I was a street dealer.'

Walter is under no illusions about the crime situation on the Costa del Sol. 'It's very dangerous here. A lot of the gangs rely on drugs for nearly all their income and yet the price of drugs is plummeting and that's making the dealers even more protective of their turf, which in turn means more guns being fired.'

Walter says he's definitely noticed an increase in violent incidents between gangs. 'These people are fighting for their lives, literally. They have no other way of surviving.'

Meanwhile, back in Benalmadena's 24-hour square Frankie and his gang are still available at all times of the day and night to supply drugs to anyone willing to pay. He says he is counting down the months until he quits crime but it's tricky to see how he will ever escape such a life unless he gets carried out in a wooden box.

It's difficult not to get depressed in this part of Spain. Unfinished building sites dominate the skyline. Shops and bars are closing at the rate of a dozen every week as the recession bites harder and harder. It feels almost like a ghost town compared to what it once was. Much of it has become a dead zone just hanging onto survival but unsure how long it can really survive in its current form.

The reality on the Costa del Sol is a lot worse than I ever expected. Crime is definitely on the increase and gang violence is escalating at an alarming rate. The gap between rich and poor is getting bigger because the boom years are over and the crock of gold and the sunshine that attracted so many people out here in the first place are long gone.

Hugh is one of a dying breed on the Costa del Sol. He's seen it all over the past ten years: the gang feuds, the scams, the threats, the victims and the police. They've all presented themselves to Hugh at some time or another. Hugh isn't directly involved in any of this stuff but he knows all the players and he knows more than most why the Costa del Sol has turned into such a deadly battleground for gangsters.

'It's getting worse and worse out here. The clever old-timers have stepped back and allowed the younger, more erratic villains to take all the flak. The trouble is that these characters are not the real thing. They don't pause for breath and they don't seem to appreciate that guns are only for show. You simply don't ever use them. You just scare people with them.'

Hugh, from south London, now runs a 'club' called Maxim's in Fuengirola, where men pay women for sex. It's all above board and Hugh is not directly connected to that side of the 'business'. As he said, 'The girls are free to do what they want. They're nothing to do with me. I just run the bar area.' About a dozen girls, mainly from South America and eastern Europe are based at Maxim's and among the best customers, says Hugh, are policemen and 'businessmen'.

But even Maxim's sometimes finds itself playing host to

the sort of trigger-happy young hoods who have turned this part of the Spanish coast into such a dangerous place. 'A place like Maxim's is always going to attract gangsters. It's the very nature of the place but on the whole they are usually very well behaved, although it's quite clear looking at them that some of the younger ones are right on the edge of exploding and they are usually the ones who get caught up in the crossfire so often.'

In the daytime, Hugh also runs the infamous London Pub right on the beachfront at Fuengirola where many of the local 'faces' drink at night. 'This place is teeming with villains but it's no big deal,' he said. 'These sorts of people are vital to the income of the town. They spend a lot of money and places like Fuengirola could not survive without that 'black' economy.'

The prostitution scene in Fuengirola and on the whole of the Costa del Sol is kept carefully out of sight from the millions of tourists who visit every year but it is well known to residents and regular visitors. It can be perfectly summed up by Hugh: 'In Latin society there is absolutely nothing wrong with a man going to hookers for sex. A lot of Spaniards come in here on their way home from work, take a girl to a room, pay her one hundred euros, buy her a drink, sleep with her and then continue on home to their wives and kids. It's the norm out here.'

And yet, ironically, it's this openness towards sex that has caused some of the tension between various gangs of criminals out here on the so-called Costa del Crime. Small-time 'runner' Eddie explained: 'I know it may sound crazy but a lot of young villains come here and wander straight into the nearest knocking shop and fall in love with a hooker. It's complete madness. Then there are huge battles between some young gangsters and their rivals over women. Typically, much of this is fuelled by over-use of cocaine.'

Meanwhile, Maxim's governor Hugh takes a philosophical view of the whole melting pot of crime on the Costa del Sol: 'We all know there are loads of psycho bunnies out there vying for territory but as long as they don't hit any innocent civilians then most people don't really care.'

Hugh says he has witnessed many classic encounters between some of the coast's heaviest villains. 'Up to a few years ago most of the heavyweight characters were Brits and they always went out of their way to keep this stuff away from the prying eyes of normal people. Trouble is now the foreigners are involved and they don't seem to care who gets hit in the crossfire.'

Hugh believes that many of the 'real criminals' who've been settled out here for years will move on soon. 'A lot of them are sick and tired of all this shit. They just want to earn a crust and keep a low profile, but it's not easy to do that when you've got young kids sticking AK-47s up people's noses. I think in the end it'll be an even worse free-for-all out here, which will spell real trouble for everyone including the so-called innocent bystanders.'

5

THEY SAY THAT on the Costa del Sol there are only two types of criminals: the ones who survive and the ones who end up in a wooden box. Paul Grimshaw is not a criminal but he has had his finger in a lot of pies, and he has witnessed at first hand the gang wars here. Northerner Paul first arrived on the coast more than ten years ago without a clue as to the sheer depth and nastiness of some of the British criminals operating down here.

Then he got involved in a business that looks after Brits' holiday homes while they are back in the UK and soon got to see some of the 'activities' that gangsters get up to, all in the name of crime. 'I've seen the worst of the worst and they are completely out of control down here,' explained Paul.

'It was like something straight out of *The Sopranos*,' he said. 'A lot of these characters were behaving as if they were a law unto themselves and they were surrounded by trigger-happy cocaine-addicted thugs ready to shoot anyone if ordered to do so.'

Despite being a thoroughly law-abiding citizen, Paul found himself witnessing increasingly disturbing incidents. 'I am a pretty straightforward sort of bloke and some of this stuff was bloody scary. And I knew I'd have to do something.'

Today Paul says certain British gangs have turned their operations into virtual 'businesses' so as to have legitimate companies fronting out all their criminal activities. Many gangs own restaurants, estate agencies and chains of bars as well as currency exchange booths in many city centres along the coast, where much of their cash can be easily laundered. 'A lot of people know the gangs behind these businesses but no one raises an eyebrow. Mind you, they'd be shot dead if they did.'

When the big gangs came into 'contact' with any of their opposition numbers among the other big Brit 'teams' on the Costa del Sol, 'measures' were always taken to ensure that they knew who was charge. Paul explained: 'Every now and again a few smaller operators came on the scene not realising just how powerful these big boys were. Then a couple of soldiers were dispatched to "have a word with them". There were two brothers from Yorkshire causing a lot of problems one time and they just disappeared one night and were never seen again. Some believe they were killed; others are convinced that they left the country immediately because they were so terrified of what would happen if they stayed.'

Another pair of brothers who arrived on the Costa del Sol penniless but who soon amassed an estimated £50 million fortune from drugs were the M's from just south of Manchester. Their 'reign' of terror, which based in Calahonda – between Marbella and Fuengirola – is still talked about to this day.

At one stage it was estimated they were knocking off gang rivals at the rate of one per month in a bid to ensure other villains lived in complete and utter fear of them. Debbie, from Stoke, worked for the M's for five years and not surprisingly she only agreed to grant an interview for this book if I assured her of complete anonymity. 'They'd slit my throat if they knew I was talking to you,' said Debbie at the quiet beachside corner café where we met. 'Those two brothers are the most evil people I have ever met in my life.'

But, says Debbie, like so many other Brit 'criminals' on the Spanish coastal areas, the M brothers arrived in Spain as 'complete nobodies'. She explained: 'Let's call them Mickey and Dave. They arrived as kids in their early twenties having been run out of south Manchester by some very notorious gangsters. And you know what? As soon as they touched down here they announced they were big-time criminals and started bigging it up around all the usual bars and clubs where the other British criminals go. They told me later it was all bullshit but it was part of their plan to set themselves up and make sure no one crossed them.'

Debbie met the brothers when she had a brief affair with the older brother, Mickey. She explained: 'I was a silly young bird from the Midlands and I was quite impressed by Mickey's gold teeth and his clever banter with women. He swept me off my feet but then I came crashing down with a bump when I found out he had three other girlfriends. We stayed friends, which was a miracle in itself.'

The brothers decided that Debbie was trustworthy and asked her to run an estate agency business they set up to help launder the proceeds from their drug-running activities in

Spain. 'I knew what they were up to but it was a well-paid job so I went for it. I suppose back then I actually believed they weren't such a bad pair of fellas.'

But 18 months after starting work for the brothers, Debbie went through a chilling experience, which convinced her the brothers were completely out of control. She explained: 'I was out on a date with a new boyfriend and we bumped into Mickey at one of the best restaurants in Fuengirola. We all sat down together and had a brief chat and a drink, then went our separate ways. I was actually quite surprised at how civil Mickey was to my new boyfriend because he'd always seemed like the jealous type. Anyway, I thought nothing of it until two days later when my boyfriend called to cancel a date we had arranged for that night. He sounded very nervous but I thought nothing of it at first. Then he stopped answering my calls. I eventually bumped into him in a bar in Benalmadena and he completely ignored me. I was so angry I went up and had a right dig at him. Then he virtually burst into tears and explained that two "friends" of Mickey's had visited him at work the day after we'd all met up and told him to never see me again. He was absolutely terrified because they threatened to kill him if he disobeyed their orders.'

Debbie continued: 'I was completely outraged and went straight round to see Mickey that night to demand an apology. Mickey just laughed in my face and tried to seduce me on the spot. I slapped him in the face and stormed out of his house saying I never wanted to work for him or see him again. Next morning I went into the estate agents' to get my things and Mickey was in there laughing about it all and saying it wasn't anything personal and why didn't I just forget everything that was said and get back to work.

'But I told him I couldn't work for him again after what had happened. I then started shouting at Mickey in front of all the other staff about his criminal activities and how he should watch his back. Well, the whole place went silent and I realised that I had probably overstepped the mark but it was too late to back down.

'Mickey then got up and walked out of the office without saying another word. Everyone else just looked at me as if I was completely mad. I had dared to confront him and now it was dawning on me that I might be his next victim if I wasn't careful. I grabbed all my stuff and walked straight out of there. As I drove off I passed Mickey in his Mercedes just sitting there watching me drive by. It was bloody frightening. I felt he was trying to give me a message but I never actually heard from him again, although I spent the next few weeks expecting a visit.'

Debbie believes the only reason she got away with insulting Mickey was because he had a soft spot for her and he was obsessively polite to women in general. 'Like so many criminals, Mickey adored his mum and he said he always tried to treat women as politely as his mum would expect him to treat them. He said he could never harm a woman, although I took a lot of that with a big pinch of salt.'

Debbie has never set eyes on the brothers since then, although she says that for two years she had to keep away from all her regular Costa del Sol haunts in case she bumped into them. 'I heard they were very angry with me for quitting on them because people just didn't ever defy them. But I guess I was permitted to live because I was a woman.'

She then went on to reveal some of the inside secrets of the gang wars which these two brothers have been waging against their criminal rivals on the Costa del Sol since the mid-1990s. Debbie explained: 'Like so many others, I'd heard the rumours about how Mickey and his brother Dave were chopping rivals up but I didn't take much notice of it until just before I had that fallout with them. I came across a small-time coke dealer called Alfie who operated out of Benalmadena and occasionally supplied me and my pals with a gram of Charlie. Well, Alfie was very scared when he happened to hear I worked for the brothers. One time he sat and had a drink with me and told what had happened to his cousin who had worked for Mickey.

'It turned out that this bloke's cousin was spotted talking to a Spanish copper in a bar. Within a day he'd been taken up into the mountains, shot in the mouth and buried alive. I didn't believe this story at first but then I was back at the office one day when Mickey was around and I heard him talking about this bloke and how he was 'up in the mountains now' and I knew at that moment he must have been buried just the way his cousin had described.

'Then I came across other people who had similar stories about how Mickey and his brother Dave were like homicidal maniacs, chopping up and shooting business rivals who got in their way at the rate of about one a month. I started noticing how certain people did seem to be disappearing. I knew it must be true and I also knew what Mickey was capable of. He was the coldest person I have ever met in my life. And he even seemed quite happy for all these stories to circulate because it made him a figure of fear on the coast. In other words, no one would ever dare take him on.'

The brothers have recently slipped off the Costa del Sol radar but Debbie believes they've simply stepped back from the criminal spotlight 'because they've made so much money they can let others take the big risks from now on'. Debbie explained: 'Mickey and his brother were at their peak about five years ago. They ran loads of straight businesses off the back of their drugs empire and seemed untouchable.'

At one stage they were 'very friendly' with a well known British TV personality who lived on the Costa del Sol. Debbie takes up the story: 'This TV star was a complete pot head and he scored all his drugs from Mickey. Trouble was he was often broke and ended up owing Mickey a huge amount of cash.

'Well, after about six months of free credit, Mickey decided this TV star fellow was taking the piss and he would call in the debt. The celeb was completely freaked out, burst into tears and claimed he was so broke he couldn't pay Mickey any of the money he owed. Mickey had that fellow doing a live act at one of his clubs for numerous nights on the trot for free to pay back what was owed. Mickey must have made so much money because his club was packed out every night and no one knew the real reason why this bloke was even appearing on the stage in the first place. After that, he quickly moved back to the UK to get away from Mickey, even though Mickey would never have had him hurt because he was too high profile.'

Clear evidence that kidnapping is coming back onto the criminal agenda out here on the Costa del Sol came in January 2009, when a 76-year-old Spanish 'businessman' called Fernando Moreno Espada was snatched from his home in Marbella and found dead the following day near a local reservoir. One Spaniard and three Colombians from a notorious crime gang were later arrested in connection with the kidnapping.

Police later revealed they believed the kidnapping had been intended to raise €1 million but the gangsters' plans went wrong and they panicked and killed Señor Espada. His body was found gagged and with his hands tied behind his back in a deserted building near the main A7 motorway. Moreno had had a long career in the construction industry and owned a local cement factory plus a number of estate agents.

A few days after the Espada kidnapping, also in January 2009, a 35-year-old Irish gangster called Richard Keogh was riddled with bullets in a Benalmadena street, signalling an alarming escalation in gangland violence on the Costa del Sol. Keogh had already been hit three times by bullets in a previous attack but this time his killers clinically finished him off with cold-blooded impunity.

Keogh was a well-known criminal face along the southern Spanish coastline. He'd fled his native Dublin a year earlier after another attempt on his life in County Meath, Ireland.

As another Irish villain in the area told me just days after the Keogh attack, 'This fucker had it coming. They'd been chasing him years. It was only a matter of time.'

Keogh, married with four children, had only just moved to Benalmadena from nearby Alhaurín de la Torre (ironically, just a stone's throw from the main prison mentioned earlier). Keogh was in a local bar near the busy coastal main road with two associates when he went outside and was approached by a man. Seconds later shots rang out and he fell to the floor still conscious. But then, according to witnesses, the gunman closed in on his victim and finished him off with four more shots to the face and upper body. The hitman's stolen Honda Civic was found in the nearby Torrequebrada area with the keys still in the ignition; smoke was coming from one of the seats, which implied that the gunman had thought he had set fire to the car before abandoning it.

The police attitude towards killings between criminals on the Costa del Sol is worth mentioning here. One of Marbella's most senior detectives told me a couple of years ago that he simply didn't have the manpower to investigate such crimes. And as if to prove the point he pulled out the police file on one of the Costa del Sol's most notorious unsolved killings – the shooting dead by a hitman of ex-Great Train Robber Charlie Wilson, in 1990. Fifty-eight-year-old Wilson was gunned down in the garden of his own home just beneath the mountains behind Marbella. But that file contained *just two pieces of paper*. The detective explained: 'We can't waste our time on this sort of thing. If criminals want to shoot their rivals dead that's fine by us because it means one less gangster out on the streets committing crimes.'

Charlie Wilson had been up to his neck in major drug deals on the Costa del Sol so the expat criminal community were far from surprised when he was murdered. 'He was the classic victim of two gangs falling out,' explained one old crime vet who still lives a stone's throw from Charlie's hacienda in the hills behind Marbella.

'Charlie headed up his own little team and then these younger villains turned up and started trying to muscle in on his territory,' continued Wilson's erstwhile neighbour. 'Well, Charlie wasn't the type to take that lying down but he never envisaged they would carry through their threat to kill him. The young blokes behind that murder were sending out a message to all the other older gangsters on the Costa del Sol to watch their backs. A lot of the older characters actually retired soon after Charlie's death because they recognised that all the old rules no longer applied and it was better to get out while you were still alive.'

The killing of Charlie Wilson focused more attention on the activities of the old-time British villains who'd settled in alleged 'retirement' out on the Costa del Sol. It gradually became clear that many of these ex-bank robbers and blaggers had turned to drugs as the main source of their income from crime.

Wilson's murder probably single-handedly helped a new breed of gangster start to make his mark on the Costa del

Crime. The old-timers stepped back to a certain extent, shocked by the cold-blooded nature of the attack on Wilson. In their place came cold, hard, calculating young men, many of whom were permanently hyped up on coke and who took absolutely no prisoners.

It was only in the late 1980s that Spanish police first realised the huge scale of British drugs-smuggling operations on the Costa del Sol. More than 60 per cent of all hashish on the UK streets arrived from Morocco, and a lot of it came courtesy of a Brit called Brian Doran. Instead of going straight to the Rif mountains, where the marijuana is still grown to this day on neat terraced farms hidden in cedar forests, the Doran gang relied on Moroccan middlemen that they visited regularly in the plum-coloured, carpeted lobby of a Tangier hotel. Like other big 'firms' still operating to this day, Doran employed a 30-strong team of boatsmen, drivers, electricians and heavies – men 'good on the beach' – who unloaded the hashish bound for British markets. Rarely did they bother with quantities smaller than half a ton.

The hashish was usually stashed inside the panels of a huge lorry in a Moroccan warehouse. Then the lorry would be loaded with perishables such as oranges, frozen fish or flowers and sealed shut with a Transport International Routier (TIR) bond, which would insure that the cargo sped through Spanish, French and British customs checkpoints along the road. The Doran gang also transported the hashish by ship, and this was how the British smugglers were finally caught. Following a tip from Scotland Yard, the Spanish police put a telephone wiretap on Scotsman Doran's Marbella villa. One night, the firm's motor cruiser, *Retaliation*, was scheduled to pick up a load of hashish at a Moroccan beach near El Jebha. But in the dark the boat's pilot kept missing the beach. Exasperated, he docked and rang Doran asking for better directions. The Spanish intercepted the call and sent an armed launch out to meet the *Retaliation* after it finally found the right beach and had scooped up the haul.

Unfazed, Doran's remaining men began flying the drugs from the Rif mountains to a small airfield near Mojácar, in Almeria province in south-east Spain. But he and 11 others were eventually arrested after an undercover police operation which ended up with the authorities confiscating a ton of hashish, a grand villa, as well seizing the plane and 14 vehicles, including the obligatory Rolls-Royce.

As a result of Doran's arrest many spin-off British gangs started up, using carriers or 'mules' – who can strap up to four kilos to their body – posing as tourists on the charter flights home. The going payoff was a thousand pounds a carry – or, if caught, seven years in jail.

Also, after the break-up of Doran's 'firm', the other gangs on the Costa del Sol learned to be more cautious. These days, the TIR lorries are often given an escort of cars whose drivers can warn them of police blockades or, once they enter the UK, fend off ambushes by rival gangs.

It's all run very efficiently, almost like a legitimate business. Crime Inc is certainly thriving on the Costa del Sol.

6

GREAT TRAIN ROBBER old Charlie Wilson would no doubt have turned in his grave if he could see what has happened to his beloved Costa del Sol in recent years. A lot of criminals have joined forces with gangsters from other countries in order to survive. When, at the end of 2006, a multinational crime gang was smashed by police, two Bulgarians, three Lebanese, five Moroccans, three Algerians, a Brazilian, an Israeli and a French citizen were arrested. The gang preyed on wealthy foreign tourists on the Costa del Sol and was suspected of carrying out at least 500 robberies in hotels and villas, as well as cloning credit cards.

Meanwhile, drug gangs continue to use murder as a way to exert more power and influence on the Costa del Sol. Irish drug gangs were blamed for the brutal murder of a notorious Dublin villain called Patrick Doyle, gunned down in his car near Marbella in early 2008. Doyle met his match while he was travelling in the front passenger seat of a BMW 4x4 driven by a man called Gary Hutch as they headed towards La Cancelada, outside Estepona.

As Doyle chatted on his mobile phone, a gunman emerged from a 'green car' blocking the way and fired four shots through the windscreen of the BMW. Attempting to flee, driver Hutch could only crash into a lamppost. As the two men tried to escape on foot, the gunman singled out Doyle. Remarkably, Doyle managed to stagger from his car to a nearby alley, but another gunman, who'd arrived on a motorcycle, calmly dismounted, followed him and shot him twice in the head at point-blank range, while a Spanish family and Hutch looked on. Another notorious figure in the Dublin underworld was dead. Spanish police later revealed that two hit teams – using a 4x4 and a motorcycle – had been following Doyle.

At least 13 bullets were fired at Doyle, who died at the scene. A terrified Hutch, meanwhile, crouched in terror and waited until the gunmen had left before presenting himself at a local police station. Hutch was the nephew of notorious crime figure Gerry 'The Monk' Hutch, who, for many years, had ruled the criminal hinterlands back in Dublin, with the aid of a sawn-off shotgun.

Doyle was renowned as an enforcer and was thought to have been involved in a long-running feud between two south Dublin drugs gangs that had claimed several lives. He was also a right-hand man to Freddie Thompson, a drug baron also associated with Dublin's gang wars.

In Ireland, the police at first claimed that a Russian Mafia hitman shot Doyle dead acting under orders from his locally-based leader, whose close relative the 27-year-old Dubliner had beaten up. But Doyle had been the chief suspect in at least two murders carried out in his native Dublin in 2002 and 2005. He had eluded the Irish police, the Garda, and gone on the run via Liverpool and Manchester, eventually ending up on the Costa del Sol. From there he helped run a drugs empire, smuggling vast amounts of cocaine from Spain into Ireland.

While Doyle's murder had initially been blamed on the Russian, it was then linked to a gangland murder in Amsterdam four weeks earlier. Doyle was said to have been contracted to kill a British drug dealer but had shot the wrong man. His intended target decided to retaliate before the next assassination attempt.

In fact, Doyle had been hiring himself out as a contract killer from his hide-out in Marbella. It was an ideal location for him because of the large Irish community in the area and he liked the many British and Irish bars and clubs. Within 24 hours of Doyle's murder, officers from the Spanish Police's Drugs and Organised Crime Unit arrived at his villa on the outskirts of Estepona. Suspects had been seen moving furniture from the property. After searching the premises, the police found 115kg of high-quality cocaine hidden in the furniture. It had a street value of €7.7 million. An Irish national was among those arrested. It was then revealed that Doyle had been on his way to meet a British criminal when his car was ambushed, and this triggered speculation that his death was most likely linked to the drugs haul.

Back in Dublin, one police source explained: 'Doyle was typical of the third generation of gangland "soldiers" from Dublin. He was aggressive, showy and started fights at a whim. He and his ilk are unlike the older Irish criminal types on the Costa, who live a very quiet life and just get on with their business.'

Doyle's murder was a major blow to his gang as he was regarded as the most ruthless member of the group. His mistake was that he believed he could earn a 'hard man' reputation in Spain, but he was in fact regarded as nothing more than a minor criminal figure by the international traffickers using the Costa del Sol as their base.

It even emerged that Doyle had been unable to flee Spain for Ireland because of another contract on his head over the murder of rival gangster, 27-year-old Noel Roche. Doyle's DNA had been found on the 9mm handgun used to murder Roche outside a yacht club in Clontarf, Eire, in November 2005.

Police believe that three of Doyle's henchmen were near the Estepona gym when their boss was shot. But none of them could respond when Doyle's car, driven by Gary Hutch, was ambushed. Within hours of the Doyle killing his gang were in hiding, fearing they could be targeted next.

Just a week after Doyle's cold-blooded murder, a former member of the drugs gang led by legendary Dublin underworld boss John Gilligan had to undergo surgery to have bullets removed from his shoulder. Peter Mitchell, 39, originally from Summerhill in Dublin's north inner city, was wounded twice in a gun attack near Marbella. Mitchell had left Ireland shortly after the murder in 1996 of the journalist Veronica Guerin and the inception of Ireland's Criminal Assets Bureau.

Spanish police made a lot more effort than usual with this incident because two other men wounded in the shooting were bystanders and not the intended targets. The men, in their forties and seventies, sustained wounds after the masked gunman targeting Mitchell tripped and fell while he was trying to flee.

Many Irish gangsters on the Costa del Sol believe the big turning point for them came back in 2000 when armed men dragged Dublin drug gang boss Michael McGuinness from his home near Marbella. He even left behind a very reluctant witness – a terrified hooker. The unnamed vice girl was not harmed and raised the alarm after the kidnappers drove McGuinness away in his own Range Rover. McGuinness's body was found two days later in his car at Málaga Airport. He'd been bound, gagged and shot in the head twice at close range.

Security guards at the car park were alerted by passers-by who noticed masses of flies and a stench coming from the Spanish-registered vehicle. The police reckoned McGuinness ran foul of the Mafia and other organised crime figures in the area. His death was clearly a warning to other Irish and British crime lords involved in the vicious turf war that had first kicked off in the mid-1990s. McGuinness was classified as a businessman but had been under police surveillance during the previous year for suspected drug-running.

The police later said McGuinness had come to their attention on fraud-related charges rather than as a drug dealer. McGuinness's property company carried out a number of business deals with a firm partly owned by Dublin crime boss Mattie Kelly. There was also talk of money laundering for gangs on the Costa del Sol.

But the Costa del Sol had already become more than just a sanctuary for Irish criminal fugitives. Many gangsters involved in murder, drug dealing and smuggling actually relocated there for operational reasons. Among them was Christy Kinahan, an armed robber turned international drug dealer who had been freed from Portlaoise prison. Sean Dunne was another who made the move after he was shot outside his home in Ratoath in County Meath. He already owned a number of properties in southern Spain and was facing a €4 million tax demand from the Criminal Assets Bureau in Dublin.

Gennádios Petrov, the alleged head of the Tambovskaya-Malyshevkaya Russian crime gang, was detained in June 2008 on the Costa del Sol. In a big police operation, code-named Troika, 20 members of the gang led by Petrov were arrested in Majorca, Málaga, Alicante, Valencia and Madrid. Police seized €200,000 (£178, 000) in cash, 23 luxury cars and a Dalí painting. Bank accounts containing €414 million were frozen. Mr Petrov and 17 others were charged with a variety of offences including money laundering, murder, extortion, drug-dealing, illicit association, falsification of documents and tax fraud. The arrests were the latest in a string of police operations targeting the illicit activities of the

Russian Mafia, many of whose leading members have moved their entire operations to the Costa del Sol in recent years.

This particular Russian Mafia gang was said to be 'one of the four biggest in the world', and had been using Spain as a base for its top leaders and for money laundering its gains from illegal activities in Russia and other former Soviet states.

In November 2001, police on the Costa del Sol arrested 18 members of a Lebanese criminal gang on suspicion of supplying money and arms to militants in the Middle East. They believed the gang raised money for the soldiers by forging credit cards, robbing tourists and making fraudulent timeshare real-estate deals, mostly with Britons and Germans. The group allegedly raised €8 million, but police did not say how much of it went to the Middle East.

In June 2007, Spanish police arrested three Russians, suspected of assembling and masterminding a transnational gang, whose World Wide Web swindles brought in more than half a million euros, removed from many bank accounts. The gang, which also included two Estonians and a Dominican, had its HQ in Britain, with branches in Spain's Catalonia, Valencia and on the Costa del Sol, and accomplices in the USA, Australia and New Zealand.

Not long after these arrests, Spanish police extradited a suspected Georgian crime gang leader called Zahar Knyazevich Kalashov after he was arrested in Dubai coming out of a party attended by other Georgian and Russian criminal gang members. Spanish police had been searching for Kalashov since arresting 28 suspected gang members in 2006. They were accused of money laundering, fraud and other crimes.

In that operation more than 400 officers staged raids in 11 cities along Spain's Mediterranean coast. Some 40 homes and businesses were searched as part of the raids, and 800 bank accounts frozen. The suspects allegedly laundered money from criminal activities in the former Soviet Union by investing it in real estate, restaurants, bars, luxury cars and other assets in Spain.

In 2007, Spanish police claimed they had broken up 29 Costa del Sol organised crime gangs and arrested hundreds of people suspected of crimes ranging from drug trafficking to forcing women into prostitution, but the reality was that this was no more than a small drop in the ocean. Authorities said the detainees were nationals of Spain, Morocco, France, Britain, Colombia, Nigeria, Russia, Romania, Germany and China. Other crimes they were of accused of included money laundering, arms trafficking, fraud and kidnapping.

And in the middle of all these gang wars, the notorious Colombian drug barons were trying to turn Africa into a hub for shipping cocaine to Europe. Lured by Europe's high demand for cocaine, the strength of the euro and lax law enforcement in poor African countries, Latin American drug gangs began 'setting up shop' in Ghana, Nigeria, Guinea-Bissau and Ivory Coast in the continent's west and Kenya in the east. In the case of cocaine, they began to ship the drug ready-to-consume by boat to Africa and then sent on to Europe by land, plane or ship. Meanwhile, traffickers were still also using other more traditional smuggling routes, with Spain remaining the main gateway for cocaine entering Europe.

It was a busy Friday evening in July 2007 at The Point, a bar in Marbella, as the mainly British clientele enjoyed the warm night air on a terrace overlooking a palm-tree-lined golf course. Among the drinkers was a regular known as Gerry, a popular 43-year-old Londoner who'd been living around the British-dominated neighbourhood of Nueva Andalucía for some years. His real name was William Moy.

In the few seconds it takes to pump half a dozen bullets into someone from point-blank range, the calm of an idyllic Mediterranean evening was shattered. 'There were several shots and everybody just hit the ground,' said one person who was in The Point that night.

By the time people had picked themselves up off the floor or begun to run, a blood-spattered, bullet-ridden Moy was either dead or close to dead. An ambulance crew certified his death at the scene.

Speculation immediately started that the increasingly deadly battles being fought by British drug gangs in Spain had erupted among the bougainvillea-clad villas and white-painted, low-rise apartment blocks of Nueva Andalucia. 'They say it was a gangland execution,' said Romualdo Velasco, a local shop-owner whose apartment overlooks The Point. 'The British keep themselves to themselves, so it's hard to know.'

There was no doubt that the gunmen wanted Moy dead. He had taken at least five bullets. A rumour doing the rounds of the Costa del Sol's British pubs in the wake of the shooting was that Moy's wife and children may have witnessed the killing. Other reports spoke of three men who were either drinking with him or who appeared at his table.

Up until then, The Point had not been one of those joints that are known haunts for British crooks, and it was clear that, whatever the motives for William Moy's killing, he was going to be missed. Nowhere was this more apparent than on the cards on the bunches of flowers outside the bar. 'I will always love you My Baby, forever and ever,' one read, concluding: 'And I will be with you one day my son. Love Mummy.'

In all there were two-dozen floral tributes wilting in the sunshine outside The Point. Messages on them described him as 'a great mate', 'a dear friend' and someone 'who will never be forgotten' and 'constantly in our thoughts'. They were signed by people like 'Little John', 'Biff and Family' and included the names of numerous British couples and families.

Spanish police, who carted the corpses of four executed British and Irish crooks off to morgues in that same month of July 2007, were keeping tight-lipped. But William Moy was already well known to the police across Europe as a major gangster.

The Moy killing marked yet another disturbing development on the Costa del Crime. 'It used to be that the British fought in other ways,' said one local. 'It was the other foreigners killing one another. But now we have noticed the

British are getting violent in a way that they were not before,' he added. 'Now they have – and use – firearms.'

Then, just a few weeks later in August 2007, a 38-year-old Estonian man was also shot dead at The Point. He had connections to organised crime and worked as an installer of saunas on the Costa del Sol. While sitting at the bar he was shot in the back of the neck by one of two men who arrived on a moped. The attackers, whose faces were hidden under helmets, escaped. Police described the shooting as a professional hit.

The victim had been living in Spain for at least a year and enquiries linked him to a gang connected to organised crime. A close friend of the victim arrested in February 2006 was one of the main leaders of the gang and believed to be linked to the kidnapping of a British national in Benalmadena two years earlier.

The Costa del Sol was clearly in the middle of yet another vicious drug war. Even before the second shooting at The Point, a security guard at another Marbella club was shot five times in a bungled hit as coke barons wrestled for control of the area. The target was a Liverpool hood and his shooting came after yet another murder, this time of top drug smuggler Colin 'Smiggs' Smith, in November 2007. Gang sources in Marbella later claimed Smith was killed on the orders of another drug baron called 'The Bird of Prey'. The pair were jostling for control of Smith's 'turf' – Puerto Banus, near Marbella. It was even rumoured that gangsters loyal to Smith were out for revenge and that team included a group of former IRA hitmen known as The Cleaners.

In November 2008, there was yet another shooting at the renowned Nikki Beach Club in which a pitched battle was fought between gangs while crowds of onlookers watched in shock. A man was shot in the leg during that incident.

In March 2005, the reign of one of the world's most powerful gangsters came to an end on the Costa del Sol. Millionaire gambler Brian Wright was at the centre of an international manhunt for ten years after allegedly leading the most successful cocaine smuggling gang to target Britain. He'd also been linked to several killings and a British horse-race fixing ring. Irishman Wright was alleged to have made more than £100 million from drugs. The fugitive drugs lord had only just moved to Spain from Cyprus and he was running all sorts of criminal enterprises from his base near Marbella.

Between 1996 and 1998, cocaine worth an estimated £300 million was smuggled into Britain by Wright's gang. They only came unstuck for the first time in 1996 when one of their boats was caught in a storm and forced to dock in Ireland. Customs officers in Cork searched the ship and found 599 kilos of cocaine, worth £80 million. A subsequent surveillance operation over the next 18 months uncovered a huge drugs business importing up to 300 million pounds' worth of cocaine by boat into the UK from Spain.

7

EVERY NOW AND again, the police on the Costa del Sol
actually pull their fingers out and nick someone. That's what
happened back in 2001 when a freed UDA killer was
arrested along with three other Belfast men in a raid on a
Costa del Sol apartment block. The former terrorist had
skipped to Spain with his family after rumours reached the
UDA that he was an informer. He'd earlier been convicted of
the murder of 19-year-old Adam Lambert in Belfast but was
given early release under the Good Friday Agreement.

Jimmy Harbinson, 35, had already been arrested earlier
that year in Belfast following a drugs seizure, believed to
have been worth £2,000, in Glengormley. He was freed on
bail but went to Spain and was arrested alongside well-
known brothers Donald and Gary 'Mummy's Boy' Marno
and 37-year-old Alasdair McKendrie.

Detectives later netted two sub-machine-guns, a handgun,
handcuffs, a small amount of drugs, cash and 'a pile' of
forged Irish passports and ID documents when they swooped
on a villa in Torremolinos, just along the coast from
Fuengirola and all the other better-known Costa del Sol
resorts. Spanish police even claimed the men had been
involved in a failed attempt to kidnap an Englishman who

had drug convictions. A Fuengirola police patrol car came across a gang trying to force the man into the boot of a car, but they escaped. Officers are also investigating whether the men had any links to the murder of Michael John McGuinness, whose body, as mentioned before, was found tied up in the boot of that Range Rover at Málaga Airport.

One of the first cold-blooded hits in Marbella was back in 5 October 1996, when a French couple was murdered in an apparent gang-warfare attack in Marbella that shocked the local criminal community. Jacques Lambert, 45, and his wife, Catherine Isabel Gastana, 37, were shot to death and another French citizen was wounded in the attack at their luxury chalet.

Three gunmen entered the couple's villa at night and opened fire with machine guns. Police said the killings appeared to be the result of a settling of accounts between French criminal gangs. The couple were allegedly connected to a hashish-trafficking ring between north Africa and France. Three weeks later police arrested eight people in connection with the shootings.

A year earlier, in 1995, the so-called 'Tin Can' drug gang had flooded Scotland with cannabis smuggled in cans from the Costa del Sol. Gerry 'Cyclops' Carbin and Mick Mackay were caged for six years each for a massive operation to smuggle the drug to the country. Carbin, 39, from Castlemilk, Glasgow, told judges in Málaga that he was entirely responsible for the drug ring, and Mackay, 32, of Cathcart, Glasgow, admitted working for Carbin. Carbin was known as 'Cyclops' in the Costa del Sol underworld because he was blind in his right eye.

Before the raid he was regarded as Scotland's biggest drugs mover in Spain. His gang was said to have raked in £100,000 from each smuggling run. Two other Scots, including one of Carbin's brothers, were also sought. Carbin himself spent three years in a Spanish jail as a result of the grisly 1990 murder of a Norwegian disco owner. He was released untried and was extradited back to Glasgow to face trial for cocaine dealing. He was later acquitted.

Just to give you an idea of the sheer scale of murder and mayhem caused by the Russian gangs, here is a chilling statistic: when Spanish authorities liaised with the Russian police to bring two Moscow-born crime lords to justice in 2003 they immediately cleared up 44 unsolved murders. When apprehended, Sergei Butorin and Andrei Pylev were running drugs, prostitution, money laundering and teams of hitmen. No wonder the old-school Brit gangsters try their hardest to avoid any contact with the Russians.

By the summer of 2008, the drugs war between gangs on the Costa del Sol reached frightening proportions as determined British, Irish and eastern European gangs stepped up their deadly battles. In August that year, two gangland shootings took place in Marbella within 48 hours. The price of drugs continued to drop so gangsters needed bigger quantities to make the same profits. But there were lots of gangsters and only a fixed quantity of drugs – and that's when the clashes turned deadly.

There are some legendary British names who try to stay in the shadows of the Costa del Sol. Patrick Adams, the eldest of the notorious Adams brothers, a north London family linked to crime, moved to Sierrezuela on the hilly outskirts of Fuengirola some years back, after he was acquitted of involvement in a £26 million cannabis deal in Britain. Adams kept a low profile and his favourite watering hole, Gilligan's, was a modest window-less drinking club on the road to Mijas behind Fuengirola. It offered live racing via satellite television as well as Guinness to carefully selected guests. If you were not on the list you'd get no further than the heavy metal doors. Adams's two children went to a prosperous international school nearby, and he and his wife lived in a house with high whitewashed walls covered with bougainvillea and bristling with security cameras, buzzers and infrared body detectors. Local police had had Adams in their sights for years, and first compiled a surveillance report about him as far back as 1995. But he never put a foot wrong.

Towards the end of the 1990s, the British and Spanish police beefed up their operations on the coast, setting up special units against drugs and organised crime. Skilled in foreign languages and phone tapping, they were ready to pounce on those suspected of drug trafficking, money laundering or – increasingly – outbursts of gang violence, as clan wars were settled in methods reminiscent of the era of Al Capone.

But it seems that until the recent worldwide financial meltdown, the old-time villains were masters of discretion. They opened restaurants and golf resorts so as to cover their tracks, knowing that if they broke the law they'd be flown back home, but the new younger bunch of criminals moving onto the Costa del Sol were far less cautious.

In 2005, a 3-year operation by Spanish police and British Customs officers came to a dramatic close when Timothy O'Toole, an Irishman a British passport, and several others were arrested for cocaine smuggling. A trawler, reportedly supplied by O'Toole, was apparently headed for the Irish Republic when it was intercepted near the Canary Islands. On board was about 3.5 tons of cocaine, worth over €150 million. O'Toole was sentenced in a Spanish court to 15 years in prison.

The civil guard police force (guardia civil) in Málaga, the regional capital, has over the years conceded that it does not have the manpower to check each of the 15,000 Interpol inquiries received each year concerning European gangsters on the Costa del Sol. Only last month Michael Walsh, 62, on the run from Britain since March 2000 for alleged drug trafficking, was tracked down to his villa, but only after being spotted with other suspects.

On the same coastline, police arrested 13 suspected gangsters accused of laundering £75 million made from extortion, drugs and killings, by buying hotels, property and art treasures.

In November 2005, Spain demanded the extradition of three members of a Birmingham-based family of Indian origin who were alleged to be involved in a suspected drugs and crime gang on the Costa del Sol

Seven Britons were arrested in southern Spain and another six were detained in Britain as part of the same investigation. They included Kuldip Singh Sander, 44, his brother Malkit Singh, in his 50s, and Kuldip's nephew, Narvinderjeet Singh Sander, 29 – all originally from Perry Barr. The Spanish police suspected Kuldip of being a leading member of a gang, which allegedly smuggled cocaine and cannabis to Liverpool and Yorkshire and laundered millions of pounds through airline and clothing businesses in Birmingham. The suspects were believed to have had global links to other money launderers. The profits were also channelled through shady property deals on Spain's south coast.

During police raids, property and bank accounts worth £34 million were seized along with £103,000 in cash, jewellery and designer watches, 2,100 cartons of contraband tobacco, false passports, and seven cars including a Jaguar, Mercedes, BMW and Chrysler. Eleven firearms including rifles and shotguns were also found in the raids. Police also froze assets worth 'tens of millions of euros'. The outcome of the extradition request is, as yet, unknown.

In March, 2005, police on the Costa del Sol claimed to have cracked one of Europe's biggest money-laundering rackets, which was connected to a string of international crime gangs dealing in drug smuggling, prostitution and contract murders. The police operation, named White Whale, focused on Marbella and netted 41 people including Spanish, French, Finnish, Russian, Ukrainian and British nationals. More than 250 properties were seized in the raid, which took place after 18 months of investigation. A number of bank accounts credited with millions of pounds were frozen. Properties in Marbella, Mijas and San Pedro de Alcántara were among those raided. A conservative estimate of the seized assets in Spain alone was £200 million.

In May 2006, Spanish police arrested eight alleged leaders of a Costa del Sol timeshare fraud scheme, accusing them of defrauding 15,000 people. The gang had been operating since 2000 and made profits of €18 million. The men arrested included four Britons, two South Africans, one from Belgium and another from Norway.

In a statement police said that the gang used more than 300 shell companies and over 1,000 employees to carry out the alleged fraud. Among other things, the criminals contacted people who owned timeshare property and offered to help them sell it, persuading them to pay money for notary fees and taxes for a transaction that was never going to take place. The gang also sold timeshare slots it did not possess to more than one person, and in cases when it was actually handling a property, sold it to several parties.

The gang even posed as a collection agency, offering legal proceedings to help people who had been cheated by the gang's own bogus firms!

Yet many gangsters continue to feel so untouchable on the Costa del Sol that they use their homes in southern Spain as bases from which to organise worldwide crimes. In June 2005, a drugs gang who plotted to import cannabis worth £11 million from Cambodia and Laos through West Yorkshire were jailed for a total of 38 years. Ringleader Daniel Redmond, 60, from Dublin, had plotted the international operation from his luxury home on the Costa del Sol. A string of his accomplices, several from West Yorkshire, were jailed and fined thousands of pounds after West Yorkshire police officers risked their lives to go undercover to smash the smugglers.

In December 2003, two brothers from Merseyside who escaped from prison after being convicted of a plot to flood Australia with drugs were rearrested on the Costa del Sol. Gary Murphy, 35, and Andrew Murphy, 29, from West Kirby in the Wirral, were allegedly involved with a gang who were stealing luxury cars. They were also accused of smuggling 'any type of drug' – including hashish and cocaine – back to the UK.

Five years earlier, in October 1998, a two-year investigation by British Customs and the National Crime Squad led to Gary and Andrew Murphy being sentenced to ten years each at Liverpool Crown Court for conspiracy to export drugs and conspiracy to launder almost £1 million of the proceeds. They masterminded a 12-strong gang who plotted to smuggle ecstasy and amphetamines into Australia inside the heels of women's shoes.

More than 100 pairs of shoes were recovered from a luxury Wirral apartment owned by a property company called Watermark Developments, which had been set up by the Murphys. The heels of the shoes were cut away and filled with amphetamines. But the prison life clearly didn't suit the brothers, who escaped from HMP Sudbury in East Anglia. It eventually turned out that Spanish police had had the two Murphy brothers under surveillance since February 2002.

In March 2008, a bunch of Costa del Sol police officers made the headlines for all the wrong reasons. Four inspectors from an elite unit that combated organised crime in Málaga were charged with bribery, embezzlement, dereliction of duty, ownership of illegal arms, and revealing confidential information. Forty officers were questioned in connection with the case, which related to alleged payments received by Russian gangsters for reports on police surveillance operations. One officer was also alleged to have delivered an envelope containing details about the girlfriend of a Russian who was arrested for cocaine smuggling in the US.

Back in late 1999, an Irishman with a bullet wound in his stomach was one of an armed gang, which forced a former

British soldier to bring cannabis worth £150,000 from Málaga. Jack Burns, who served in Northern Ireland, and Dean Matthews, an electrician and disc jockey, were eventually jailed for three years at Dublin Circuit Criminal Court. Burns, 28, a native of Easterhouse, Glasgow, Scotland and Matthews, 30, formerly of Kidderminster, England, pleaded guilty to importing cannabis at Dublin Airport when they eventually appeared in court.

Burns, who had an address at Sitio del Golf, Mijas Golf, on the Costa del Sol, claimed he was forced into the crime by threats to his family from gang members who said they knew he had served with his regiment in Northern Ireland. Matthews had borrowed £600 from one of the gang, a man called 'Gary', the one already mentioned, who had the bullet wound in his stomach. Shortly before being ordered to take part in the drugs run the ex-soldier was beaten up by 'Gary' and another man, and told his debt was now £900.

It was yet another typical Costa del Sol crime story. It's almost as if the sun helps breed the criminality that dominates so much of the life out here.

8

IN JANUARY 2004 the stakes changed dramatically when a British police officer was stabbed while carrying out surveillance of gangs on the Costa del Sol. A second officer was wounded slightly after the pair were attacked and stabbed during a working trip to the coastal resorts. The National Criminal Intelligence Service (NCIS) later admitted that the seriously wounded officer – who was believed to have sustained kidney damage – and his colleague were attacked after having supper in a restaurant in Fuengirola. A Spanish police officer with them was also stabbed by the attackers as they were preparing to get into a taxi outside the restaurant in the Los Boliches area of Fuengirola. The two NCIS officers had only been in the Costa del Sol for a short while as part of a coordinated action against British crooks living in the area.

The attackers consisted of at least two men of Moroccan or Algerian origin who had also been at the restaurant. An off-duty Spanish police officer who had been dining at the restaurant gave chase, but the attackers got away. The perpetrators had been sitting at a table outside the restaurant and had stabbed the men 'without saying a word'.

Then in March 2004, things turned even more dangerous on

the Costa del Sol when a British businessman was kidnapped in Marbella. His family eventually paid a ransom believed to be more than one million euros for his freedom.

Millionaire property developer Frank Capa had spent nine days tied and bound at an unspecified location on the Costa del Sol. The elderly Londoner – said to be an acquaintance of both Rod Stewart and the former EastEnders star Michael Greco – was kidnapped close to his home on an exclusive development near Marbella. Spanish police later confirmed that between four and six armed men in balaclavas blocked his car with two vehicles and bundled him at gunpoint into a jeep.

The gang of kidnappers, believed to consist of Britons and Lithuanians, had earlier followed Capa from his home as he drove to his golf course in a new silver Bentley GT. The dramatic kidnap sent chills down the spines of the area's many wealthy residents. 'A lot of us are very worried and taking extra precautions,' said Capa's friend and fellow businessman Frank Boyd at the time. 'Frank was a decent family man, with children. I've known him for 25 years and I can't understand why anyone would do that. I guess he's been doing really well and just got unlucky. His mistake, if he made one, was driving around in fancy cars, and he certainly has a few of them. Put it this way, a lot of us are swapping our gold Rolexes for steel ones.'

Police believed the gang was targeting rich foreigners who showed obvious trappings of wealth. 'It seems there are quite a few groups of former soldiers from the Eastern Bloc, highly trained but with no money, who are prepared to carry out these sorts of crimes,' said a Málaga police source at the time. 'It's not a difficult crime to commit and with so many Russians and eastern Europeans now flocking to Spain it is difficult to identify them quickly.'

Capa was said to be 'well but shaken' after his ordeal. His kidnappers were never apprehended.

Running a successful drug gang on the Costa del Sol requires a big 'investment' of cash, and this is why some of London's richest old-time bank robbers have been in demand down the years. The Moroccan go-between usually takes 50 per cent upfront for his merchandise. The boatmen rake off another €100 for every kilo shipped across the Strait of Gibraltar, and the cost of yachts, refrigerated lorries and villas raises the expenses even more.

But for an investor back in the late 1980s and throughout the 1990s, the returns were enormous. Like any enterprising businessmen, smugglers always try to diversify their product. Back then the main drug-smuggling connections for cocaine on the Costa del Sol were made through Argentine criminals, who transported the white powder down from the Andes and on to Spain via Buenos Aires.

At that time, the big gangs had perfected the old Mafia murder technique of coating their victim's feet in cement, taking them out to sea and dropping them overboard to sink. There were other 'methods' too. One gangster explained to me how one suspected 'squealer' was dealt with: 'This grass was invited out on a night run across the Straits (of

Gibraltar). He was in the cabin when we came down screamin' that a Spanish patrol boat was on its way. We had him hide in a sleeping bag and pull it over his head. Then we just tied the top of the sleeping bag so he couldn't fight his way out and chucked him overboard. Like drowning kittens. Simple, innit?'

Back in the late 1980s and 1990s, Spanish police failed to penetrate any of the British gangs because few of them ever hired any Spaniards. Recruitment was carried out back in the UK, relying on the traditional family and social networks that existed long before even the Krays and the Richardsons popularised the image of the flash Cockney family gangster.

In March 2005, a murder hunt was launched on the Costa del Sol after the bodies of a Briton and his wife were found at their £500,000 villa in Spain. The 68-year-old man had told neighbours he was a former East-End gangster with links to train robber Ronnie Biggs. The male victim's body was discovered in a pool of blood outside his home. He was naked from the waist down and had knife wounds to his back and legs. His German-born wife was inside the villa, which had been destroyed by fire.

Drugs and vice are not the only criminal activities on the Costa del Sol. In late 2008, hundreds of Britons were feared to have fallen victim to a £50 million sting in one of the biggest scams ever perpetrated in Spain. Police swooped on offices in the resorts of Mijas and Fuengirola and 20 suspects were arrested. Those being questioned faced charges including fraud, falsifying documents, money laundering and tax evasion. Many of the 2,000 investors in the company were British and they lost all their cash as a result of the firm luring investors through property exhibitions, cold calls and mailing lists.

In May 2008, 55 Nigerians were arrested in Málaga in armed swoops by Spanish fraud-busters on more than 60 homes and businesses. The gang was believed to be behind a £21 million lottery con, which had fleeced hundreds of Britons. The gang ripped off 1,500 victims worldwide – many of them British – for a whopping total of £21.6 million. The Costa del Sol crackdown followed the jailing of a Nigerian in Surrey after a disabled British pensioner was swindled out of his £100,000 life savings in a lottery scam. Victims would get letters saying they had won vast prizes in Spain's legendary state lottery. The villains then followed up with demands for cash to cover 'local taxes' and 'administrative charges'.

But this was just one of numerous white-collar crimes on the Costa del Sol which have been attracting the interest of gangs in recent years. Teams of villains have been filing false robbery reports in order to make claims on their insurance; more than 100 people were arrested by Málaga police in connection with such scams in 2008 alone. Police reckon the financial meltdown will force even more gangs to try and cash in on these blatant insurance fiddles.

Over the past 25 years, Marbella has in many ways become Europe's answer to Miami. The sprawling, warren-like *urbanizaciones* of the Costa, where neighbours speaking dozens of different languages rarely meet, and front companies own many properties, provide perfect cover for all sorts of illicit activities. As Europe's internal borders came down in the mid-nineties, gangsters found they could drive unchallenged from Palermo, Marseilles or Amsterdam to Marbella, and the Costa del Sol experienced an increase in the violence. Spaniards, alarmed by the bloodshed, called it 'La Costa del Plomo', or The Lead Bullet Coast.

One of the most infamous killings of the 1990s was that of well-known Marbella lawyer Francisco Bocanegra, who had connections in the former Soviet bloc countries. Bocanegra's body was found in August 1996. His Bulgarian murderer, a member of an international homosexual prostitution ring, was eventually jailed for 17 years. The Bocanegra family was part of Marbella's establishment and his murder sent shock waves through the community.

A year earlier, in August 1995, a Russian loan shark, his wife and their seven-year-old daughter were killed in their luxury villa in the Nueva Andalucia region of Marbella. Their half-buried corpses were discovered in nearby Casares. Another Russian, Ivan Ivanov, was later given three 28-year sentences for the killings. The spate of violence raised real fears that Spain was already in the middle of a deadly gang war. In 1997, alarmed by the Costas' new-found reputation for violence, the Spanish Government set up a special police unit whose job was to track and control the gangs. Police officers with a special knowledge of languages and computer technology were chosen to join the elite corps, known as the UDYCO, or National Police Drug and Organised Crime Unit. Newspapers began to talk of a new breed of super-cop and of 'Marbella vice'.

At the police headquarters in Málaga in the late 1990s – where the UDYCO was based – Comisario Jefe Antonio Ramírez spent much of his time carefully checking through Interpol paperwork on wanted Costa criminals. Outside his office window, officers in the jet-black outfits of Spain's police assault teams practised abseiling into action.

Much more recently – in January 2008 – the Irish police were looking into the rumoured demise of yet another Spanish-based Dublin drug gang lord. Rumours were spreading that Freddie 'Fat' Thompson, leader of one of the feuding Drimnagh/Crumlin gangs, had been assassinated in Spain. Thompson had been warned several times by the Irish police about threats to his life. The 27-year-old had been in Estepona, on the Costa del Sol, the previous February when one of his close associates, Paddy Doyle, also 27, was shot dead. The murder was never solved but Spanish police reckon Doyle – and Thompson – had run foul of Turkish drug traffickers.

Thompson travelled between Dublin, Amsterdam and the Costa del Sol. He was arrested in Rotterdam in October 2006 when police seized seven kilos of cocaine, six handguns and ammunition at an apartment he had been using. But he evaded prosecution on a technicality when the case came to trial in February 2007.

Thompson was also an associate of Martin Foley, who'd been the target of several murder attempts. The latest had been in January 2008, when he survived after being hit by five bullets. The gang feud in which Thompson and Foley were caught up began in 2000 when a gang of young drug dealers from the Drimnagh-Crumlin area of Dublin fell out after the Garda seized cocaine found in a hotel. The gang split and the violence started with the murder of one of their number in 2001. Since then there had been nine more murders, dozens of attempted murders and hundreds of violent incidents.

Associates of Thompson said the murder in Spain of his friend Paddy Doyle had badly affected him and he had been acting in an erratic manner ever since. Doyle had been Thompson's main 'enforcer' and had personally carried out the assassinations of two of Thompson's rivals.

Spain's CESID secret service was the first to warn that the Russians were going to invade the Costa del Sol in the mid-1990s, as bundles of roubles began to appear at casinos. 'Marbella is an important centre for wealthy Russians, who use it to rest from their illegal activities,' said one senior investigator.

Estate agents, luxury-car salesman and police officers all began noting that the Russians, criminals or not, had extraordinarily large amounts of cash and insisted on only buying the best. Luxury cars with blackened windows and strange yellow numberplates could be seen cruising Marbella, parked at Puerto Banus, or pulling up beside yachts in the up-market Sotogrande development, 40km to the west.

Russian businesses in Marbella sold either luxury goods or sex. In Puerto Banus, where the suntanned, designer-clad crowd pushed its way past the rows of Rolls-Royces, Mercedes, Porsches and Corvettes, the harbour-front designer boutiques stayed open until midnight. Just around the corner from a Russian-owned lap-dancing bar, sat another legacy of the Russian mob. The cream-coloured hull of the *Joselle* motor-yacht stretched into the bay, its deck and radar carefully covered with protective rubberised sheeting. This boat belonged to Alexander Sigarev, a crooked Russian banker wanted for stealing £50 million from his own clients at Moscow's Novbusinessbank. After his bank collapsed, he installed himself in a mansion in the exclusive Las Chapas area of Marbella. His first move, apart from buying a Gibraltar-registered Rolls-Royce and the *Joselle*, was to hire the protection services of Russian 'mafioska' gangster Leonid Terekhov. But Spanish police were tapping Terekhov's phone and discovered he was running his Moscow-based 'Medvekovo' crime syndicate by remote control from Marbella.

When Sigarev eventually (and inevitably) fell out with Terekhov, the gangster turned the tables on the billionaire. He flew in a team of hitmen from Moscow's Izmailovo crime family. At a meeting in Puerto Banus, bugged by the

UDYCO, an imported thug called Vadim Tichomirov ordered the banker to hand over £5 million 'or else'. The Spanish police then swooped and arrested 13 Russians and impounded Sigarev's yacht.

One of the most worrying facts about the Sigarev case was clear evidence that the Russian banker had already established contacts with Marbella's notoriously corrupt town hall, obtaining special licences for land around his property. The town hall was at the time run by mayor Jesus Gil, a swaggering, bullying right-wing populist. The anti-corruption department of Spain's attorney general's office later claimed that Gil used Marbella for business deals in which municipal funds – those of his Atlético Madrid football club and his own bank accounts – were treated as part of the same empire.

But then Gil was a man with blood on his hands. Thirty years earlier he'd spent time in prison after a hotel he built illegally, without architect's plans, collapsed. Fifty-eight people were killed. Spanish dictator Francisco Franco released him, and Gil went on to make a fortune out of real estate and construction deals. On his office wall was a painting of a scene from *The Godfather*.

Even Marbella's courts had a reputation for being riddled with corruption back in the 1990s. Gangsters, including several Brits, made unproved claims that bribes were being taken to release people on bail or to shelve cases. One prominent judge's brother was a business partner of three Italians identified by police as members of the Catanian Mafia.

In July 2005, suspected Russian Mafia bosses were arrested on the Costa del Sol in the biggest operation against money-laundering in Europe. Spanish police detained 28 leading gang members believed to have been involved in an operation to launder money through coastal tourist resorts that are popular with Britons buying villas there.

Numerous properties were seized by police, while others belonging to foreign buyers faced demolition after it was discovered that gangsters bribed local councillors to build them. Undercover agents involved in the sting, known as Operation Wasp, also seized art treasures, jewellery, cash, luxury cars and guns in their weekend raids across 11 regions. The gangs allegedly funnelled cash from extortion, drugs and prostitution in Russia into fraudulent commercial and financial networks, including their property portfolios.

In October 2006, Spanish police responded to fears that British gangs were widening their international operations by mounting a campaign to round up fugitives hiding on the Costa del Sol. Those sought by British police in Spain included escaped prisoners, murder suspects, drug traffickers, fraudsters, counterfeiters and robbery suspects. Any information deemed useful would be passed on to Spanish police, who'd execute the arrest warrants and send the suspects back to Britain.

A hotline was even set up in Spain for British expatriates to call with anonymous tips on the whereabouts of ten people listed on a new 'Crimestoppers Costas' website.

As a result, in June 2005, three British men were arrested

in an undercover operation near Marbella that smashed one of Europe's biggest cocaine-smuggling rings, worth £360 million. Then Scottish millionaire gangster Pat McCadden, nicknamed Pat the Rat, was arrested in Marbella on suspicion of shooting a police officer. Earlier, in 1985, he'd been jailed for ten years after a £600,000 heroin haul.

Working on information from the Scottish Drugs Squad, Spanish police officers put a remote villa in the mountains behind Fuengirola under surveillance in April 1997. Eventually armed officers using helicopters swooped on the villa. Donald Mathieson, 35, and Robert Gillon, 40, from Glasgow, and Keith Barry, 40, were caught red-handed unloading 11 sacks of hashish from cars – this had a street value of around £2.5 million. It was destined for a specially adapted bus which had been built in 1996 at a cost of £52,000 at a Carlisle coachbuilders and afterwards, in the Glasgow area, was converted to carry drugs. The gang had adapted the vehicle by raising the seats, which left an 18-inch gap underneath the floor aisle. The bus is believed to have been used to smuggle drugs worth millions of pounds out of Spain over a number of years. A British couple who run a bar in Torremolinos said, 'The bus used to come here twice a year. There were about a dozen kids always accompanied by four adults.' It seemed that the drug smugglers wouldn't hesitate to use children as cover for their activities.

During the 1990s, gangs running prostitution rackets on the Costa del Sol continued to go from strength to strength, with eastern Europeans gangs already beginning to make great inroads. Back in 1996, a 27-year-old Scots woman from East Kilbride went to work in Spain as a barmaid and ended up being forced by one of these ruthless gangs to work 12 hours a day as a prostitute. She was only freed after the brothel in Mijas Costa near Fuengirola, where she was held prisoner, was raided by police.

Pimps had stolen the woman's travel documents, fed her cocaine and heroin and sold her to a Romanian gang, who repeatedly raped her before putting her to work in brothels. She effectively disappeared and news of her fate only came out when this was disclosed by other girls who remembered working with her.

It's believed there are more than 150 such brothels operating on the Costa del Sol employing foreign girls. Many of their young victims come to Spain on the false promise of working as a dancer, waitress or singer in the area's clubs.

The gunmen lay in wait as their prey parked, before riddling the car with bullets. It was September 2007.

Two of the passengers were killed immediately; the third died later in hospital. The dead, all Colombians, were the latest victims of gangland hits on the Costa del Sol, raising fears that a new crime war had erupted. But then these Colombians were not looking for a quiet life. They were ready to spill blood in their ruthless pursuit of profits from the multimillion-pound cocaine trade. Spain's Central Brigade for Organised Crime estimates that between 20 and 30 Colombian gangs with at least 300 members operate in Spain and they continue to instil fear in their criminal opponents on the Costa del Sol.

As one old-timer explained to me: 'The Colombians are highly professional and completely ruthless. The only way to stop them is to kill them and that's what happened when those three died. The trouble is it will never scare the Colombians away from Spain because they've got plenty more soldiers where that lot came from.'

It seems that the Costa del Sol is at the centre of a seemingly never-ending circle of crime. Illegal activities help to fuel the economy so the perpetrators' power and influence just keeps on growing. There is, quite simply, no way to stop it.

COSTA BLANCA

Costa Blanca investigative writer and former club owner Danny Collins has encountered many of the gangsters currently battling it our on his 'manor'

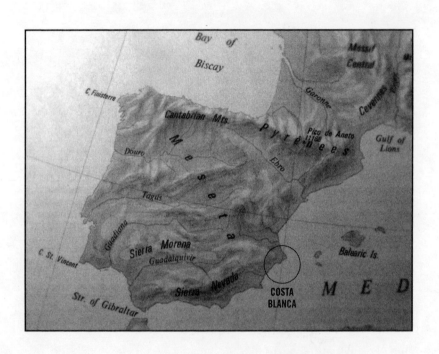

9

BENIDORM IS UNDOUBTEDLY the crime capital of the Costa Blanca, on Spain's eastern coast. But it also happens to probably be the only place on earth with a square named after a soap opera – Plaza Coronation Street. This high-rise nightmare on the Valencian coast is also famous for its nightlife. At Carriages cabaret bar, on Calle Gerona, a character called 'Sprightly Stevie Nelson' is likely to start a Monkees sing-along and 'Dangerous Ricky Dale' is notorious for his Cliff Richard impersonation. When you're tanked up on sangria, pop next door to K-Tattoo and get a pit bull inked on your arm.

About 65km south of Benidorm is Torrevieja. Eastern European criminal gangs came to this seaside resort, halfway between Alicante and Cartagena, in the 1990s and liked the place so much they bought whatever properties the Irish criminals hadn't already snapped up. Holiday guides will tell you that the town has a salt museum, a friendly working harbour and lovely white-sand beaches. They don't mention that despite a 40 per cent drop in reported incidents, the town has the highest crime rate in Spain.

By the beginning of 2005, Irish drug gangsters as well as former IRA and Northern Irish Loyalist paramilitaries had turned Torrevieja into the base for their multimillion-euro illegal operations. Numerous gangsters – including members of the emerging west Dublin gangs – had invested proceeds from armed robberies and drug sales in local property in the area.

By that same year – 2005 – more than half of the 85,000 population of Torrevieja were foreign nationals and many of them were law-abiding Irish and English couples in their forties and fifties who'd paid out thousands of euros on second homes for investment or pension purposes. Not surprisingly, these homeowners were becoming more and more uncomfortable at the sight of increasing numbers of Irish criminals in clubs and bars. Torrevieja's booming property trade had also seen the appearance of the Russian Mafia, as well as Moroccan and expatriate English narcotic dealers, all of whom were eager to expand traffic routes for the transit of hard drugs.

Police sources in Ireland suggest that some lesser-known criminals were using the booming residential market in Torrevieja to disperse some of their combined ill-gotten gains. And besides, there were undoubtedly many attractions to living in Torrevieja.

Few of the big-time gangsters' faces are well known in the city, giving them greater freedom to operate. Also, Alicante airport is just 30 minutes' drive away and the city boasts 320 days of sunshine a year, which means temperatures that rarely fall below 15°C in winter.

But then the Costa Blanca throws up some unlikely gangsters with a lot of 'previous'. One of the characters I met on my travels across Spain proved a gold mine of information when it came to the British gangs on the south-east coast. Bob Webster has got a finger in every dodgy pie on this coastline. This 65-year-old from south London wears loads of chunky gold jewellery on his fingers and around his neck, and he favours a thick beige cashmere overcoat, which does make him stand out from the beach crowd in the sleepy seaside town of Javea, half an hour north of Benidorm, right in the heart of the Costa Blanca.

'There's a war going on down here but all the tourists haven't got a clue because it's all about criminal versus criminal,' says Webster. He has numerous businesses including restaurants and an estate agency but he also freely admits he's operated on the wrong side of the law for most of the thirty-odd years he's been a resident in Spain. His overview of the gangsters who operate in these parts is worth hearing.

'I was one of these hoods for a lot longer than I care to admit,' Webster told me. 'It's a cesspit out here, with different classes of gangsters coming onto the scene in droves.' Webster sees the Costa Blanca as being split into different criminal subdivisions.

'You've got the scumbags of Benidorm, where they'd kill their own granny for a tenner and I call them the Gas Meter Bandits. Most of them are young idiots trying to scrape a living. They're completely fuckin' out of control.

'Then you've got Torreviejo which is a strange town a long way off the beaten track, which the Irish and eastern Europeans have turned into their second home. It's not a very nice place and the property has always been cheap there but it's become the centre of operations for the Paddies and they're the biggest nutters of all. Then you've got places like this, Javea, where there is a classier type of criminal operating. We get a lot of Russians here and they only deal in big quantities of cash, although they are as cold as ice, so if you cross them the chances are they'll come back and kill you.'

Webster says he's come across 'all sorts'.

'The Costa Blanca has got 'em all. Car thieves, fraudsters, kiting cheques, money laundering and then of course the biggest earner of all – drugs.'

As Webster spoke to me in a tastefully decorated café overlooking Javea's picturesque beachfront, waiters hovered nervously, offering him clean ashtrays and a light for his cigarette every time he fiddled with his pack of Marlboro Lights. It was clear that Webster has a lot of 'influence' in this town. 'Listen,' he said. 'I've made a lot of big money out of all sorts of produce – but never drugs. I've left that to the real gangsters round here.'

He then painted a picture of trigger-happy villains who have turned this 100-mile strip of coastline into a cesspit of crime. 'Everyone keeps banging on about the foreign gangsters doing this and foreign gangsters doing that. Well, let me tell you, son, the British gangs are still out here, still shooting at each other and the foreigners, and still raking in the cash. They're just as hard as the rest of 'em.

'The foreigners have done us a favour in a sense because they've taken all the attention away from us so we can get on with the art of making money and they take a lot of the flak.' Webster took a long drag of his cigarette before he continued. 'I've had to sort people out, threaten a few with violence and take the law into my own hands on a number of occasions but no one comes after me now because they know I will not take any shit from anyone.'

Webster then recalled a recent incident, which sums up the level of gang violence that exists on this stretch of coastline. 'I know this British gangster who owns a business near here and two young hoods tried to lean on him for some protection money. The next thing I know one of them's been found floating in the sea, apparently he'd drowned.'

Webster says Spain's recent property crash has made a lot of gangsters even twitchier. 'They've got no way of laundering their cash in property like they used to. They're getting desperate and when that happens it gets even more dangerous.'

The wily old one-time gangster – who calls himself a 'retired criminal' these days – says that he won't hesitate to take on the gangs whenever they try leaning on him. 'They all know my background and that I'd have 'em over as soon as look at them if they tried anything on me.'

Webster says that recently two Irish gangsters tried to force him to pay protection money on an Indian restaurant he owns in Javea. 'Fuckin' cheek. These two men in green, that's what we call the Irish round here, strolled into my restaurant, asked to have a word and made it clear they wanted some protection money or else the building might be damaged or set fire to. Well, I lived in Limerick many years ago and I know what these sorts of characters are all about, so I stuck a gun in their heads, literally, and told them to get off my property or else I'd be squeezing the trigger. Well, you know what? They never came back. The last thing the men in green want is a trigger-happy Brit to contend with. They want soft-as-butter businessmen who shit their pants and offer to pay them without any argument. Nutters like me are the last thing they want to deal with.'

Webster says he has encountered numerous ex-IRA and UDA men amongst the 'men in green' contingent on his stretch of the Costa Blanca. 'When the troubles ended, these characters didn't know what to do with themselves so a lot of them utilised their contacts and went into villainy full time instead of just using it to top up their fund-raising like they did in the old days.'

Webster openly admits doing a long stretch in prison back in the UK before he landed on the Costa Blanca 30 years ago. Today, he tries to keep a lower profile but admits there are so many reminders of his past just on his doorstep. 'I bumped into one of the bastard coppers who sent me down the other day just outside my own restaurant. He didn't clock me at all but I knew it was him the moment I saw him. You never forget the face of the arsehole who nicks you.'

Webster even tells a fascinating story about how the same retired detective was himself the victim of a burglary at his villa and the raiders ended up stealing £80,000 from a safe. 'Now I ask you,' said Webster, 'why would a retired Scotland Yard copper have 80,000 big ones in cash? We all know the answer to that one. It's fuckin' obvious, in my opinion. He was bent as a nine-bob note. Well, when they nicked the two kids from Benidorm who burgled this copper's place he refused to press charges. I wonder why?'

Webster says he still looks back on the eighties and nineties as the 'good old days', even though it's changed a lot. 'In the past year it's been especially hard because of the property crash. But there's still the same villains trying to make a living. There are even the same bent coppers in the Guardia Civil.'

Another Costa Blanca member of the criminal fraternity who lives in Webster's 'home town' town of Javea is a middle-aged former housewife from the Midlands called Brenda. She arrived here penniless 20 years ago with a young child and no husband. Within a year she had transformed her fortunes by becoming the main 'filter' for cocaine in Javea. A close friend of Brenda explained how she converted herself into the Pablo Escobar of this stretch of coast. 'Brenda is a very bright woman but when she first came here she didn't even know that there were any criminals in Spain,' the friend said. 'That's how green she was.

'Then she met a British bloke in a bar who suggested she might like to allow her rented apartment to be used as a "drop off" for two kilos of coke which was being delivered by boat later that same day. Brenda got paid handsomely for that deal but she soon worked out that if she cut out the middleman she could really start raking in the cash.'

Within two years of arriving in Spain, Brenda was 'running' all the cocaine supplies to Javea and the surrounding coastal resorts. 'These days Brenda will sell on coke to you in huge bundles for bargain prices but then she knows that no one else would dare to try and muscle in on her market,' added her companion.

Brenda's reaction to any rival gangs trying to 'invade' her territory are well known the length and breadth of the Costa Blanca. Her friend continued: 'A bunch of Scousers turned up here a couple of years ago and tried to set up their own coke supply route in Javea. When Brenda heard about it she sent a couple of her boys over to have a chat with the lads from Liverpool. The way I understand it is that one of those Scousers ended up with some cigarette burns on his dick and they chopped off his pinky for good measure. That was Brenda sending out a message to everyone on her turf not to dare fuck with her and it worked because no one has ever had the balls to try and take her on since then.'

Like all successful gangsters out here, Brenda made sure she was virtually untouchable by paying off the right people in power. Her associate told me, 'I know she had to give them two kilos of coke one time just to keep them on her side but she says she builds it into her profits and looks on these payments as being a bit like paying tax.'

Back to Bob Webster, the so-called 'King of Javea' for an

overview of the crime scene on the Costa Blanca that sums it all up perfectly: 'This place is crawling with vermin. A lot of people believe their own lies and fantasies over here. I think the sun and the booze and drugs go to their heads. There's a bloke round here who claims he was a driver for the Krays. Bollocks. He's never been near the bloody Krays in his life. The mistake these sort of dodgy characters make is that they believe that they can make themselves into somebodies out here and no one will notice their lies. Well that's a complete load of old bollocks. There's a lot of threatening out here but luckily not a lot of doing.'

Webster says that the gang wars here on the Costa Blanca have got so bad now that, 'The police are actually quite relieved when a villain gets knocked off or disappears because it's one less headache for them. Not long ago two British criminals fell out really badly about a drug deal and one then disappeared shortly afterwards. But instead of there being a proper police investigation into the disappearance of this bloke, the cops just swept it under the carpet and the whole case quickly fizzled out, leaving no one the wiser as to what had happened to this bloke. And you know why? Because the other Brit had a full-time Spanish cop as his partner. Now that was one hell of a clever move.'

These days Webster says he's trying to lead a 'normal' life, whatever that means. 'I do this thing where I say to myself, "The old Bob would sort that fucker out." Then I stop myself and say, "The new Bob doesn't give a fuck." That's the key to my survival these days. None of this stuff matters in the grander scheme of things and one needs to get a perspective on things. You see the "old Bob" was a bit of a psycho who'd shoot first and ask questions later. The "new Bob" is a calmer, more laid-back character. I much prefer him to the old Bob.'

Besides drugs, which still dominate the criminal fraternity here on the Costa Blanca, Webster says there are numerous frauds being perpetrated by criminal gangs. 'Mortgage fraud is the big one out here at the moment. Did you know you can 'buy' a house that's been valued at 750K for about 200K by taking on other people's debts? People are so desperate out here and yet it's a complete scam.'

Webster also believes that contrary to what many believe, the dipping price of cocaine isn't exactly hitting the profits of the main criminal players in this part of Spain. 'They just cut it with even more crap than before so they still make the same profits. It makes perfect business sense. The big-time criminals never lose out in a recession because they've always got a way to keep their profits up high.'

With a string of legitimate businesses and a toehold in virtually every corner of Javea, Bob Webster is a prime example of a classic British success story in this part of Spain. 'Look. I've never hidden my activities from anyone. What you see is what you get with me. I'm as happy here in Javea as I've ever been but that's because I've always got on with the work at hand. They say anything goes when it comes to crime but you have to have some common sense or else you end up six feet under. I'm not ashamed of anything I've done out here. I've never hurt an innocent person in my life. But why should I hide my criminal past from anyone? Out here no one cares what you're up to as long as you pay your way.'

But underneath the brash exterior lies a sensitive, highly intelligent character who knows just how far to push things to avoid being caught up in the sort of gang wars which have resulted in so many unnecessary deaths. 'The Irish have been shooting each other for stupid reasons down in Torreviejo. They're idiots. But I've always given people a chance in life. I give them the benefit of the doubt and I never judge them on their past sins. So I'm hoping the surviving Irish have the good sense to start leading a lower profile and get on with the business of making money. Killing each other over petty debts and squabbles is pathetic and it doesn't help their cause one bit.'

The Gang Wars on the Costa Blanca are summed up perfectly by Bob Webster: 'Only the strongest survive out here. The stupid little Gas Meter Operators all end up broke and moving back to the UK or dead. The crime scene is still thriving but it's like everything else; if you rock too many boats you end up drowning.'

Webster prides himself on knowing everything there is to know about his 'manor' of Javea. 'It's a mess down here in some ways. Lots of Brit scumbags and other lower level villains trying to scrape a living but they never last long. It's like a filter out here and the real operators will survive however hard the recession hits.'

Webster's own modus operandi is to: 'Make sure people continue to appreciate that I am someone not to be fucked with. I earn an honest crust these days and no one can pin anything on me. I've tried to turn my hand to just about everything out here. The Costa Blanca is my life and there are still loads of opportunities here for criminals and straight people alike, but they have to expect to fight their way up the ladder first.'

The sinister, shadowy figures whose battles continue to rock the Costa Blanca have been watched with impunity by local investigative writer and former nightclub owner, Danny Collins. He says that a lot of the biggest operators make it their business to stay completely out of the limelight, explaining, 'It's still thriving out here but the big boys keep well out of the way and use soldiers to do all their dirty work.'

Collins, who moved to a quiet, sleepy village up in the mountains behind Benidorm more than 20 years ago, says that it is still Charlie – cocaine – which seems to fuel most of the battles between gangs out here. 'Take Benidorm itself. It's full of dodgy young Brit criminals. Many of them came here as kids and have invented themselves as gangsters because there isn't much else for them to do out here.'

One of those 'dodgy Brits' in Benidorm is 23-year-old Stevie, who hails from Knutsford, Cheshire, originally but has been out here since he was aged five. Three years ago, Stevie's divorced mum moved back to the UK leaving Stevie to fend for himself. 'I'd been flogging gear since I was 15 so when my mum said she was off back home I thought I'd stay on,' he said. 'It's a good life here. I earn good money, cash in hand, and there's so much demand for coke around here that most people treat me like a God.'

Stevie has a team of five teenagers, including two girls – all Brits – working for him delivering cocaine to customers at all times of the day and night. But he admitted that in the last 18 months more and more people have been trying to take over his territory in Benidorm. 'Everyone's skint and they all think they can be villains and make a fortune. Stupid bastards. Most of them are harmless kids but now and again a couple of them get too big for their boots and try to muscle in and that's when the trouble begins.'

Stevie admitted that in late 2008, he and two of his 'soldiers' had no choice but to kidnap a rival gangster and hold him ransom to teach the 'enemy' a lesson. 'This kid was trying to take over my business so we got hold of him, tortured him a bit and then got his family to cough up 20 grand. It was a good day's business for me because he learned his lesson and kept well away from us after that and we made a shed load of cash.'

He continued, 'It's a shame we had to take those sorts of measures, but it's the only way to keep things nice and simple. I don't look for this sort of trouble. But I do respond swiftly if anyone tries to take me on. It's good if the word goes around not to fuck with me because then I don't have to bother going after many people with a shooter, which I really don't like doing.'

Stevie and his team work a lot of the most popular nightspots in the centre of Benidorm and he boasts of having at least three celebrities on his 'books'. He explained: 'A lot of the villains round here also buy coke from me and some of them are so hooked they're taking it 24 hours a day.'

Stevie freely admits he is lucky to have never been badly injured in any clashes with rival gangsters. 'This is a high-risk profession. When I was younger I expected to get a kicking now and again but these days I just want people to give me a wide berth. It's easier that way. The trouble is that when a bloke takes cocaine all day and night he gets really wired up and paranoid and that's when a lot of the trouble starts.'

Stevie admits, like so many gangsters on the Spanish Costas, that he has a couple of police in his pocket to ensure that he doesn't get hassled too often when he and his team are out at 'prime time' late on Fridays and Saturdays. 'It's just part of life out here that a criminal has to pay the cops. I have no choice. It has to be done or else me and my team would have been thrown in the slammer years ago.'

Stevie is an unusual criminal for a lot of reasons: he's well educated and brilliant at talking his way out of trouble. 'Sometimes the other villains round here, especially the Brits, think I am taking the piss when I use long words but this is me. This is what I am genuinely like. Having an education has definitely helped me to get through certain tricky situations.'

Stevie is also extremely philosophical about his situation. 'Look. I never thought I'd end up here on the Costa Blanca flogging coke and soaking up the sun. I thought I'd end up going to university and becoming a doctor or a lawyer. I still harbour a dream of quitting this job while I am ahead of the game and starting university late. I am determined to make a life for myself away from the crime scene when the time is right.'

But for the moment, Stevie is caught up in a criminal spider's web. He is earning good money and knows there isn't a job out there in the 'civilian world' that would pay him half what he is currently earning. 'I'm saving a lot of my money in the hope that when I do quit I can actually make it to university as planned,' he explained. But for the moment, he's still enjoying the rich spoils of his criminal lifestyle, which is only occasionally interrupted by quarrels with rival gangs.

'The cops just step back and do nothing. I think they want us all wiped out because that would be much easier than having to keep chasing us and following us and hoping for some evidence to put us away. A bunch of Romanian blokes came round to see me the other day saying they wanted to be my 'partner'. Well, that was a right fucking joke. They just thought they could lean on me and I'd let them take over.

'Well, after inviting them in to my apartment I asked them to sit down and make themselves at home while I prepared them all a drink. Two minutes later I marched back into the lounge with a shooter and told them to fuck off out of my flat and never return. I never saw them again or heard any more about them. I'd look on that as a job well done, wouldn't you?'

The laws of the jungle seem to apply wholeheartedly when it comes to the gangs on the Costa Blanca.

10

WHILE MANY GANGSTERS make a point of announcing a death to the world by leaving a body on the roadside, others, such as the men who shot dead Costa-Blanca villain John McKeown, prefer a body to vanish without trace. He'd last been seen drinking with friends in a bar in Moraira, a town near Alicante, in January 2007. After he was reported missing by his family, investigations by police at first concluded that he'd been killed by a British man after a drunken brawl, especially when traces of McKeown's blood were later found on furniture in his apartment, but his body was never recovered.

Then sources claimed the 48-year-old Irish drug baron – nicknamed 'The Mexican' because of his long bandit moustache – had been bumped off in Spain for having an affair with a ruthless English drug dealer's wife. Criminal sources said McKeown, from Finglas, Eire, had been ambushed and blasted to death when he returned to Spain after spending a few days in Ireland. Irish cops even flew to Spain to try and find his body.

McKeown had moved to Torrevieja, on the Costa Blanca, on his release from jail. Earlier he had been one of four men arrested on an Irish beach in July 1994 after a surveillance operation on a yacht that had travelled from Morocco.

Irish police reckoned McKeown was a 'middleman' between drugs suppliers on the Costa Blanca and the Costa del Sol. He was also linked to most of the notorious west Dublin gangs and some from the north of the city. It then emerged that McKeown was a key associate of Martin 'Marlo' Hyland, eventually gunned down by an assassin while he slept in his Dublin house.

It was believed that McKeown had been supplying Marlo Hyland's gang with cocaine, heroin and cannabis from Spain. Before that he'd been living in Liverpool – from where he sourced drugs for Irish criminals.

In August 2003, an underworld death sentence was passed on yet another of Ireland's most dangerous gangsters hiding on the Costa Blanca. Shane Coates, 31, was on the run after a shoot-out with the Irish police in May 2002, and the IRA and a rival gang had condemned him to death in his absence. Coates had 16 previous convictions including armed robbery – for which he served five years and six months – assault, firearms offences, burglaries and misuse of drugs.

Coates had crossed another notorious Dublin criminal and failed to pay off a massive debt from a drug deal. Coates then linked up with Sugg, another leading member of his 'Westies' gang, also in hiding in Spain. The notorious Westies were one of the most vicious gangs ever to emerge on the Dublin crime scene and had been heavily involved in drug dealing.

They were based in the Blanchardstown area of the city and modelled themselves on the Irish-American Westies gang that terrorised the Hell's Kitchen area of New York in the 1970s and 1980s. Coates – dubbed 'The Rat' by other criminals because of his ruthlessness and survival instincts – had even once been pictured in an Irish newspaper wearing a ski mask while pretending to strangle his girlfriend with a chain.

Coates recovered from the wounds he received in that Irish shoot-out. However, The Rat's former pals had already deserted him, fearing they'd be targeted when his rivals caught up with him. It was also known that Coates was short of cash after having to leave Ireland in a hurry, and because his assets there had been frozen he was in even worse financial trouble.

Then on 31 January 2004, Sugg, 27, and Coates, 31, went missing on the Costa Blanca. Initially they were thought to have possibly faked their own deaths, but information fed to the police by other gangsters established they had been gunned down as part of an ongoing feud with a rival gang.

Their disappearance had not been reported by their girlfriends to the Spanish police until two weeks later. The two women returned to Dublin later that year after being questioned by Alicante police.

A crack gang-busting squad of Irish police was set up specially to solve the mystery of Coates's and Sugg's deaths. Undercover officers were sent to Spain where they melted into the expat Irish and British communities in the Torrevieja area of the Costa Blanca. Well-known Irish criminals were so frequently spotted in Torrevieja by this time that ordinary Dublin holidaymakers had dubbed it 'Crumlin in the sun'.

It wasn't until two years after their disappearance that the bodies of these two notorious Dublin criminals were found in a makeshift grave in July 2006. It was as a result of Costa Blanca police digging up a lane alongside a warehouse in the town of Catral, 15km from the resort of Torrevieja and 40km from Alicante.

Police were convinced Coates and Sugg had attempted to 'muscle in' on the local crime scene, using intimidatory tactics they had employed successfully in west Dublin. But a rival Irish gang hit back and decided to eliminate their new opposition. The bodies were found shortly after 6pm following a day-long search and they remained untouched overnight while a detailed forensic examination of the scene got under way. A positive identification of the bodies using DNA techniques was confirmed several weeks later. But officers knew immediately that the torsos found in the grave, along with clothing, shoes and rolls of plastic used to cover the bodies, belonged to Coates and Sugg.

Garda sources eventually disclosed more details of the macabre deaths of the pair. They said they had received intelligence more than a year earlier that Coates and Sugg had been murdered, but did not have the exact location of the bodies. Detectives were told Coates and Sugg were brought under false pretences to a meeting in a warehouse on an industrial estate in Torrevieja. There, they were shot in the chest and upper body.

On a trip to Torrevieja a year earlier, Garda and Spanish police had identified the correct industrial estate but pinpointed the wrong warehouse, where they dug up the ground in a fruitless search for the bodies. Then the Irish police received a more detailed description which enabled them to find the exact location of the graves.

What the two Irish gangsters went through on that final journey in the car's boot, and whether they knelt on the concrete floor of the warehouse and begged for their lives, just like the addicts they had once tortured in Tallaght, will probably never emerge.

Sugg's brother, Bernard, was murdered in a Dublin pub in August 2003 when two gunmen fired six shots at him, hitting him twice. Coates had been served with a tax bill for € 125,000 by the Criminal Assets Bureau. The CAB had also slapped a bill for € 150,000 on Sugg, who had convictions for assault, burglary and armed robbery.

Within hours of the discovery of their bodies, Spanish police had arrested a chief suspect, a Dubliner wanted back home on suspicion of armed robbery. He had been on the run for five years and had been living in Spain ever since. He was later released without charge.

So gangsters Coates and Sugg certainly had it coming. They specialised in drug dealing, armed robbery, torture and intimidation. Their evil string of atrocities included the torture of a drug-addicted mother of nine. They used lighted cigarettes to burn her breasts because she owed them € 800 for heroin. When another woman crossed them they chopped off her hair and smashed up her home and car. Two other members of their gang threw a young junkie from a fifth floor balcony because he owed them €€25. Amazingly, he survived the fall and limped away.

One Garda source said there was a dispute with John Gilligan's crime gang over missing money: 'Shane Coates was given €350,000 to bring to Spain by Gilligan's gang and he was to give that money to Liam Judge (Gilligan's right-hand man, in whose 'honour' the Judge's Chambers bar is named).'

Gilligan's gang, which was responsible for the murder of *Sunday Independent* journalist Veronica Guerin, is amongst the biggest and most active criminal groups in Alicante, working in conjunction with republicans and criminals from Munster and the UK. The ex-Dublin criminal was able to call on the help of his middle-aged gangster friends.

Detectives said that bullet holes in Sugg's and Coates's clothes suggested that the men were shot in the torso before they were dumped in the grave. At least five men were involved in the double murder. An Irishman who rented the warehouse where the bodies were found was eventually arrested by Spanish police in connection with the murders.

Although Republican and Loyalist paramilitaries play an important role in smuggling everything from counterfeit-brand clothing to cigarettes and drugs from Spain to Ireland, the big players are still Dublin criminals, who are well organised and have connections to South American and eastern European crime syndicates. Not even the deaths of Sugg and Coates seemed to stem the tide of blood. The Irish gangs were virtually culling each other.

Dublin drug dealer Sean Dunne went missing shortly after arriving in Alicante in September 2004. His family insisted he had been murdered and that he was buried somewhere in the Costa Blanca. A year later, the body of Cork criminal Michael 'Danser' Ahern was discovered in a freezer in an apartment in Portugal.

It's alleged Dunne was murdered after being lured into a meeting at a local brothel. Dunne, from Donaghmede in Dublin, built up a vast property empire, much of which has been seized by the Criminal Assets Bureau but, of course, made enemies in the process. He survived after being shot seven times in late 2003 and did his best not to venture out alone again but, like Sugg and Coates, he was unable to stay ahead of the people he had crossed.

Also at this time the Irish Garda and Spanish police were particularly interested in a gang headed up by a father-and-son team, originally from south inner-city Dublin. While the father had maintained a fairly open lifestyle, the son, who was still in his twenties, was displaying all the attributes of a dedicated criminal mastermind.

When he moved to Spain originally, he chose to live in hostels or cheap accommodation, eschewing the high life – not drinking or taking drugs. He put together some major shipments of hash and cocaine – the principal drugs moving through the south-west Mediterranean from North Africa and Spain. The father, who only occasionally visited his son abroad, was responsible for organising the distribution network at home using, among others, the notorious Westies gang to shift his wares.

When one of the family's supply routes was uncovered by the Garda – who seized millions of euros' worth of cocaine at stables in Rathcoole, Co Dublin – suspicion immediately fell on 44-year-old Liam Judge, a money launderer, who was to later die of a heart attack in Alicante on the Costa Blanca. Judge 'cleaned' cash for jailed Dublin drug lord John Gilligan, and was reputed to own 20 apartments in and around Alicante, as well as a pub, The Judges Chambers, which was run by his wife Geraldine.

Mystery at first surrounded Liam Judge's fate – and relatives feared he'd been beaten to death by a Dublin drug gang as revenge for being an informer. However, an autopsy on Judge – a heavy drinker and drug user – revealed he had died of natural causes. Judge, who lived in Spain with Gilligan's daughter Tracey, 28, was also directly involved in drug trafficking. Tracey was understood to have been in Ireland when Judge died.

Judge is believed to have laundered millions for Gilligan and he also had links to the Westies drug gang based in Blanchardstown, Dublin. In the run-up to his death, Judge's affairs were being probed by the Criminal Assets Bureau.

Many Irish drug dealers believed Judge was the supergrass whose tip-offs led to millions of euros' worth of dope being seized. He went into hiding after his ex-wife Helen was kidnapped the year before from her home in Allenwood, Co Kildare.

Judge fled to Alicante together with other Irish criminals, including John Traynor and Peter Mitchell, after the murder of journalist Veronica Guerin.

Until these outrageous killings it had always been believed that there was an unwritten law in Spain that the Irish and English gangsters did not touch each other while living in their host country. The reason for this is that any murders, or other crimes, tend to attract unwanted attention from the paramilitary Guardia Civil or the civilian police, and this is bad for everybody's business.

Shortly after Judge's death on the Costa Blanca, 50-year-old Thomas Kevin Melia was arrested when police busted a €7 million cocaine ring in Barcelona. Irishman Melia was suspected of being part of a multinational gang involving Colombian, east European and Spanish crime figures.

He was arrested with a Greek man as they allegedly went to collect a €2.7 million drug delivery at Barcelona airport. Eight weeks earlier, a 40-year-old Dubliner was arrested in Alicante in a joint Irish, Spanish and Dutch operation when police recovered €250,000 worth of cocaine and a large amount of cash. The Irishman had been arrested in a hotel car park along with a Hungarian and two British men, after being tailed by police for 600km from Málaga.

The drugs were found in a five-litre wine drum in the boot of their vehicle. The Dubliner was an associate of the drug gang once led by two more notorious Dublin villains, who both died violently at the hands of other Irish gangsters.

A third success against Irish crime bosses on the Costa

Blanca came when a 48-year-old Derry man was arrested along with three others after €1 million worth of cannabis was uncovered. Police had watched the drugs arrive at Madrid airport and tracked their delivery to a warehouse in Alicante. There, they claim they found the Derry man, who police described as a former Loyalist paramilitary, helping his colleagues load the drugs into their car.

In December 2003, the police on the Costa Blanca arrested a gang suspected of taking Czech girls abroad under false pretexts and forcing them into prostitution and appearing in porn photos and films. A total of 25 girls were dragged abroad after being promised jobs as nightclub dancers and singers. Many were forced into prostitution by physical threats and psychological pressure, and then blackmailed.

Members of the gang had transported the girls to Austria, Germany and then on to Spain.

In January 2006, police on the Costa Blanca believed they had smashed an international trafficking gang involved in the importation of Class-A and Class-C drugs to the UK. Thirteen people were arrested in raids across Britain and Spain over the two days following a year-long National Crime Squad operation, which began in January 2005. Drugs with a street value of nearly £11 million were seized during the raids, including four tons of cannabis resin and a substantial heroin haul. Officers swooped on addresses in London, Manchester, Liverpool, Bristol and Plymouth, which were believed to be linked to gang members. The gang had smuggled drugs from Spain and Holland to the UK for onward distribution.

Officers from the NCS were supported by Spanish police as well as officers from Greater Manchester Police, Devon and Cornwall Police, and the Tarian Team, a drugs taskforce in Wales. Nine men and two women were arrested in Spain.

In March 1998 Spanish police arrested a 70-strong gang of motorway robbers who'd been terrorising tourists along the coastal motorway between Barcelona and Alicante for several years. The thieves, known as the Peruvian gang, targeted drivers with foreign numberplates – many of them British – who were driving south to the beaches or returning home north to the French frontier. They tricked them into stopping by standing at the side of the road and waving their arms, indicating that something was wrong with the travellers' cars or caravans – motorway resting points were often used. Led by a man called Hitler Escalante, the gang acted like modern-day highwaymen, stripping the hapless tourists of their money, credit cards and even clothes.

In fact the same gang first came to prominence back in 1990, but were rounded up and deported to their native Peru in a clampdown before the 1992 Olympic games in Barcelona.

One British victim was stopped near Barcelona as he headed for Alicante on his holiday. The same gang unsuccessfully tried to rob him again as he drove home a fortnight later. One member of the gang was arrested more than 200 times, but the Spanish authorities had initially been unable to imprison the thieves because no violence was used and the law only permitted a minor fine.

In May 2005, a British pensioner was murdered at his home in the Costa Blanca, sparking fears that violent gangs of home invaders were targeting expats. Wilson Mills, 67, died instantly when he was shot in the chest as he confronted three thieves raiding his luxury home for cash and jewels. Mr Mills and his wife Cherry, 65 – who were sitting by their pool at the time of the attack – lived in a £250,000 home on an estate along with many other Brits. Neighbours alerted police after Mrs Mills ran screaming to a neighbour shouting, 'Please, someone help me, my husband has been shot.'

A number of other violent gangs terrorised expat homeowners near Alicante for several months during 2005 and it was feared the violence was spreading. Dozens of foreign residents were gassed in their sleep and knocked unconscious so the thieves could get away with their cars, cash and other possessions. Some even awoke to discover their homes being ransacked and their valuables missing. One British man was forced to hand over nearly £2,000 at gunpoint to three men who sped off in his Porsche. Residents were so terrified that some considered forming vigilante groups to try to stop the attacks. Hundreds of Brits joined a mass march to protest about the break-ins and to demand more police protection.

Further robberies again highlighted the issue of security for many expatriates on the hundreds of kilometres of coastline from Marbella in the south to the east coastal region of Valencia. Stephen Hall, 48, a telecommunications businessman who had lived in Spain for five years, was asleep at home when he was gassed and his house robbed.

'I knew nothing about it,' he said. 'I went to bed at 2am and woke at 7am. They had stolen jewellery, computers and mobile phones. The usual.' Another victim woke up feeling groggy and staggered to the bathroom where he vomited before passing out. He realised later that morning that someone had entered his home during the night and gassed him and his family before robbing them. In reaction to the spate of crimes, residents in one development near Benidorm blocked roads leading to their estate with sandbags and mounted vigilante patrols.

Back in July 1999 a Briton was named as the suspected ringleader of a Costa Blanca drugs gang responsible for smuggling £90 million worth of cannabis into Europe. Giles Lomax, owner of a speedboat company based close to the resort of Alicante, was among 95 people arrested in a swoop by the Spanish police following a two-year probe. The businessman was allegedly responsible for a fleet of 63 high-powered speedboats used to ship cannabis into Spain from Morocco before distributing it throughout the country and into Italy and France. Police in Madrid said the gang had developed into a wide-ranging enterprise under the guise of a legitimate boating company, to smuggle at least 54 tons of hashish in the previous 24 months and to launder the proceeds. In a further link with Britain, the Spanish authorities were investigating the possibility that businesses based in Gibraltar had been used to process the drugs money.

In May 2005, a drugs baron who masterminded a plan to smuggle £1.2 million worth of drugs into Britain from the Costa Blanca was jailed for seven-and-a-half years in Leeds. Britain's National Crime Squad monitored the gang's movements and bugged telephone conversations. Gangster Ian Brennan, 36, believed his plan – which involved seven other men – couldn't fail. He was caught out by an undercover police surveillance operation. His co-accused, Graham McDonald, 42, was imprisoned for five-and-a-half years for his part in the conspiracy to import 400 kilos of cannabis resin in the back of a lorry from Spain. Brennan, described as a 'major regional drug dealer', delegated jobs to other gang members to avoid getting his hands dirty. Fellow gang boss McDonald, who was based in Nottingham, put Brennan in touch with drug dealers in Europe.

Both men jointly financed the deal, which was only thwarted when Spanish police stopped the lorry near Alicante. Brennan was also banned from leaving the UK for five years after his release from prison under a travel restriction order.

Today, one of Ireland's biggest gangsters is a man currently on the run from the Criminal Assets Bureau who lives between Alicante and Morocco. He has had close links with foreign criminal networks for over a decade and was one of Ireland's biggest contraband goods smugglers in the early nineties. He is now believed to have control of one of the biggest gateways for smuggling drugs into Ireland.

This gangster is believed to have been involved with up to ten murders in the Limerick area of Ireland in recent years. He works closely with a major drugs trafficker from Cork and both are known to socialise with leading Dublin criminals.

The golden rule for the Irish and Brit gangs on the Costa Blanca had always been to keep everything low-key. But if there were a genuine need to murder someone, it would need to involve the disappearance of the body – as was the case of Sugg and Coates and Sean Dunne, and many others on the Costa Blanca.

11

SOME GANGS ACTUALLY steer clear of drugs but still manage to make a fortune on the Costa Blanca. In September 2006, a British gang leader was ordered to repay his share of a £38 million VAT scam in a massive fraud. David Hodgson, 49, of Louth, was jailed and ordered to repay £12 million. Hodgson was one of nine criminal gang members convicted of fraud after a series of hearings at Nottingham and Birmingham Crown Courts.

The gang's scam involved a company called Intercom Espana 96 SL, set up in Benidorm in 1996, by Steven Keith Chapman, 40, of Newark, and Neil Edward Walker, 50, of Gunthorpe. Walker, a former police detective with Nottinghamshire CID, was arrested at his Las Vegas home after HM Revenue & Customs officers found him gambling illegal profits on the stock market and in casinos. The gang was sourcing mobile phones locked into the Spanish Teleffinica network and shipping them to the UK to be unlocked and sold in bulk. Their customers, major British retailers, were charged VAT, which the men failed to declare to the UK Government and instead pocketed.

Then there are the illegal booze gangs. In 1998, one bootlegging gang cheated HM Customs & Excise out of £4 million in alcohol duty over a four-year period. The gang sold 680,000 bottles of vodka, gin and whisky to outlets in northern England, Northern Ireland and Scotland without having paid import duty on them.

The gang had flourished ever since the 1993 changes to the European Union single market rules that allowed liquor to be exported overseas to leave bonded warehouses without duty being paid in this country. The gang, which included a solicitor, forged export documents and set up 'front' companies in England and Spain to give the impression the alcohol was being transported to Spain for sale. By evading alcohol duty the gang managed to undercut legitimate traders and still make a substantial profit for themselves.

Customs officers mounted a covert surveillance operation and tracked the lorries from bonded warehouses to where they were being unloaded. Bottles of spirits – identified by manufacturers' batch numbers – were found on shop shelves within days of leaving the warehouses.

But it's still primarily drugs that drive criminality on the Costa Blanca. Back in the summer of 2001, an eight-man gang of Brits were nicked by Spanish police and held in prison to await trial for their alleged part in a British drug-smuggling ring. They were said to be members of a gang trying to smuggle one ton of hashish, worth up to £6 million, on a lorry stopped near Benidorm en route to the UK.

In December 2005, a Costa Blanca lawyer was kidnapped and stuffed into the boot of his car. However, he managed to make two desperate calls for help from a mobile phone he had hidden from his captors. Carlos Reverter Ramos, 43, called the Spanish emergency number 112 and his office, telling colleagues that he had been seized. He said he thought he was being driven from Castellon, where he worked, towards Valencia on the coast north of Benidorm. He even described his two kidnappers as 'North African-looking' men.

Señor Reverter's first call to the police was just after his kidnap as he left his office. Using a tracking system, police pinpointed the call to the main road nearby. Units from the national police, the Guardia Civil, joined the hunt. Then Sr Reverter's phone signal cut out, only to be detected again about an hour-and-a-half later near a town called Almassora, close to Castellon.

The emergency services then received another call from an unidentified man who said that Sr Reverter had stopped moving. It is believed that the call may well have come from one of Sr Reverter's kidnappers, who'd found his mobile phone. Police eventually discovered the lawyer – still in the boot of his car – more than an hour later. He was covered in blood but still conscious and able to talk to police. Señor Reverter later died from multiple injuries that he suffered at the hands of his kidnappers. He was the latest victim of a new trend in Spain in which lawyers seemed to be being targeted by crime gangs who wanted to 'settle scores' with rival criminal organisations.

In October 2005 Rafael Gutiérrez Cobeño, also a lawyer, was shot four times in the head while he was driving in Madrid.

Meanwhile, Ireland's top crime-busting agency, the Criminal Assets Bureau (CAB), vowed to go after yet more gangland figures hiding out in the Costa Blanca area. Ruthless villains John Traynor and George 'The Penguin' Mitchell seemed to have been laughing in the faces of the Irish police for years, from the sun terraces of their luxury villas on the Costa Blanca.

Traynor was renowned as one of Ireland's most infamous and cunning criminals. He'd fled to Spain after the brutal slaying of crime reporter Veronica Guerin. The smooth-talking criminal, known as 'The Coach', was believed to have built up a fortune from a drugs business he ran alongside the notorious Dublin crime boss John Gilligan.

Traynor, who fed Guerin many of her stories, had always denied having anything to do with her murder. Both Irish and Spanish police were unsure if Traynor was still involved in the underworld or whether he just simply lived off his villainy after arriving in Spain.

In September 2008, rumours began sweeping the Costa del Sol that Traynor had put a € 50,000 hit out on rival Dublin crime boss Martin 'The Viper' Foley. Gangster pals of Traynor, 56, were said to have hired a North African hitman to travel to Ireland to 'get rid of him' [Foley].

They'd wanted the pint-sized mobster killed because he'd started to muscle in on their drugs turf in the Alicante area. Foley, 55, who – months earlier in January 2008 – had survived a fourth attempt on his life, was told by the Garda he was in deadly danger.

Then there was George 'The Penguin' Mitchell, undoubtedly Public Enemy Number One to the Irish authorities when it comes to crooks living abroad. Evil Mitchell was one of Europe's biggest drug barons. He fled Ireland in 1996 as the pressure from the CAB was beginning to grow. Police believed he operated between hideaways in both Amsterdam and Spain.

The Penguin was responsible for shipping huge hauls of cocaine and cannabis across mainland Europe through a network of haulage companies. He had served time in Dutch prison Bijlmerbajes for his part in a multimillion pound computer parts heist.

Gangs who were thought to be the most cold-blooded of all and manned by former paramilitaries have also set up home in Alicante since the declaration of the Northern Ireland ceasefires. Among those spotted in Alicante were brothers and former UDA men Gary and Donald Marno.

Gary, 41, and 44-year-old Donald have long been based in Spain and were, at one time, suspected of involvement in the October 2000 abduction of Liverpool criminal Thomas Rogan near Málaga. Rogan had a lucky escape when his kidnappers fled after police came across them bundling him into the boot of a car.

In June 2006, there were ever-growing fears over the spread of Latin American-style 'express' kidnappings after the snatching of a 12-year-old boy on the Costa Blanca, who was later returned to his family after they reportedly paid £34,000 for his safe deliverance. The boy was released on a country road outside the south-eastern town of Torre Pacheco, Murcia, in the early morning after being held by kidnappers for 18 hours. He'd been snatched from the offices of his parents' company by armed robbers, who had originally intended to steal wages from the safe. The kidnappers tussled with the boy's mother as they dragged him away. A neighbour saw the youngster being bundled into a van by masked men and gave police the licence number. Although police later arrested the driver and the van owner, they were unable to find the child. The kidnappers then demanded a ransom, which, as stated previously, was eventually paid.

The previous year, authorities revealed that the members of seven similar kidnapping gangs had been arrested. That year there were 147 kidnappings in Madrid alone and that doesn't include the ones that are not reported to the police.

In Madrid, gangs of Colombians kidnapped several people from underground car parks in the capital. They took as little as €700 from each of the victims, who were often left badly beaten. A woman and her five-year-old son were kidnapped for several hours in Barcelona, as was a man snatched from a phone shop.

And other gangs who roam the Costa Blanca have cost a lot of innocent people their lives in recent years. Linda O'Malley, 55, and her husband, Anthony, 42, from Llangollen, Wales, had gone to Spain to buy a holiday home in the summer of 2002. They disappeared and police eventually discovered their bodies after they had been abducted by an organised South American crime gang.

The two Venezuelans who kidnapped the British couple were jailed in 2003. Mrs O'Malley died from the stress of captivity and her husband was murdered. The kidnappers forced them to take € 30,000 out of their Spanish bank account during their week-long ordeal.

In November 2007, the brutal murder of a British pensioner by thieves on the Costa Blanca spread fear among expatriates that eastern European gangs were deliberately targeting them. Janette May Grocutt, 64, was stabbed to death as she tried to fight off thieves who were ransacking her home in the village of Paredon, near Alicante. Her bed-ridden husband Douglas heard his wife's screams from upstairs but was unable to come to her aid. The couple, who had moved to Paredon six years earlier and ran a campsite, were thought to be the latest victims of a spate of organised robberies. Gangs from Romania, Albania and Kosovo, as well as Latin America and North Africa, were targeting foreign residents and second-homeowners because they believed them to be rich. Criminals consider Britain's expats easy targets because many live in isolated villages and are not fully integrated into the Spanish community.

Mrs Grocutt's body was discovered on the floor of her home by a British neighbour. Her husband was still lying ill in his bed. Not surprisingly, Mr Grocutt – who was left uninjured by the thieves – was treated in hospital for shock.

Paredon, set in the hills and surrounded by pine forests, vineyards, olive and almond groves, is extremely popular with British expats. The Grocutts' house was particularly isolated, set in about 600 square metres of land.

Charles Svoboda, a former Canadian diplomat living in Alicante, explained: 'There is an increasing tendency for expatriates to be attacked and robbed in their own homes. The economy is not doing well and a lot of illegal immigrants find that they do not have work any more. Increasingly, you are seeing the emergence of gangs of mainly eastern Europeans, but also some North Africans and Latin Americans. For them, the expat community is easy pickings. I have heard of armed robbers targeting expats where one of the householders was kept at home at gunpoint and the other is forced to take all of their money out of the bank.'

Mr Svoboda, who runs a group offering protection for small homeowners from Spanish land-law abuses, added: 'A lot of expats either live in very isolated areas, or in built-up developments where few people live all year round. Many do not talk to each other. The British do not talk to the Germans, the Germans do not talk to the Swiss and nobody talks to the French, so you get these people who are very isolated. It's an increasingly ugly situation.'

So, the Costa Blanca's crime wave is vast and varied. Beneath the surface lies an undercurrent of criminality that seems intent on using this beautiful coastline to its own advantage. Many believe that the gang wars in this area can only get worse. Time will tell.

IBIZA

A low key property on the holiday island of Ibiza used as a drop-off by one notorious drug gang

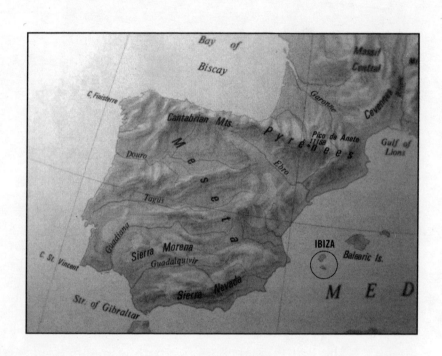

12

THE BALEARIC ISLANDS of Majorca, Menorca and Ibiza get a lot less coverage when it comes to the gang wars plaguing the Spanish Costas, but that's only because the islands are far more seasonal. In the summer holiday months, it's Ibiza – the clubbing island capital of the world – which accounts for 90 per cent of the action on the islands when it comes to crime. During the peak season months from May to September the island comes alive, and with all those party goers comes an army of drug dealers and hustlers all trying to get a piece of the action.

Since its musical renaissance in the late eighties, the tiny island (about 16 by 40km) of Ibiza has every year attracted more than half a million people, mostly under 35s. Without doubt it is the British contribution – both in numbers and excesses – that has made the island the clubbing capital of the world.

Alfredo, the Ibiza DJ who began it all, is well into middle age but still plays the island's senior clubs, the largest seven of which have a combined capacity of 23,000 – as much as the capacity for all London clubs on a Saturday night.

Some of the original English DJs claim the island has lost its glamour in recent years and don't go to Ibiza any more.

But hundreds of younger DJs do, bringing tens of thousands of die-hard clubbers, promoters, musicians, singers, and the inevitable liggers and drug dealers. And much of that drug trade is in the hands of British gangsters.

Gangster Jazzy hails from North Kensington, West London, but every year like clockwork he heads off for Ibiza to 'set up shop for the summer'. He's done the same routine for the past ten years but admits it's got more dangerous in recent times to operate in Ibiza without 'a licence'. What he means by 'a licence' is the tacit approval and permission of the drug lords who rule Ibiza and try to control the movement of drugs across the island.

'I love Ibiza. It's the coolest place on earth and I used to wish I could live there permanently but in the last couple of years it's got fuckin' dangerous,' says Jazzy. He claims that in the summer of 2008 he was personally held up three times at gunpoint by rival drug dealers trying to stop him selling 'produce' on their alleged territory. 'Until recently no one cared about stuff like that. Loads of dealers would up sticks from London and set up camp here and just rent a villa and hire a car. But it's changing. Two or three big-time gangsters are trying to run the whole island and they're quite prepared to turn it into a blood bath if they don't get their way.'

Jazzy usually rents a villa on the outskirts of Ibiza town in close proximity to the infamous vast clubs that attract tens of thousands of visitors each night during peak season. In 2006 Jazzy didn't even need to go and find the customers. They came to him. In fact most of them flew over with him. He explained: 'At least 50 of my best customers from west London come over to Ibiza at the same time in the summer so I already have a strong customer base before I even arrive there. I think that's what pisses off the drug barons. They don't like the fact that characters like me have been coming here for years and doing what we want without any interference from anyone. Professional criminals like them want to be in control of everything.

'In any case, most of my punters from London are rich middle-class media types and they don't want to deal with the psycho bunny street dealers who hang around outside the clubs here. They'd rather deal with a familiar face like me and that's why it worked so well for me to come out here.'

In the past Jazzy had direct contacts with the major suppliers of wholesale drugs on Ibiza and he'd simply put in a call from London ahead of his annual stay on Ibiza. 'It was all so easy. I didn't tread on other people's toes and there were loads of characters like me getting on with their business and keeping out of each other's way. It was what I call civilised.'

A major turning point came when a Liverpool villain known to Jazzy was shot during a gunfight between British drug gangs on the island in 2006. 'It was heavy stuff and it was a definite sign of things to come,' said Jazzy. Police later said the victim, who was driving a 4x4 black BMW X5, was the target of an attempted hit by a rival gang which was supplying clubbers with ecstasy and other drugs.

Two innocent bystanders Niall Hamilton, 18, from

Holywood, near Belfast, and his pal Gareth Richardson, also 18, were hit in the hail of bullets during the same incident. Gang member Shaun Francis Walker, 23, of Liverpool, was seriously wounded while driving the BMW. He ended up hospital in intensive care.

The dramatic shoot-out happened during a high-speed car chase through central San Antonio. That BMW X5 was later found with six bullet holes in the back and another vehicle, a Seat Leon, had three in the front. Police seized a rifle, bullets, machetes, knives and balaclavas in raids after the chase.

Later, 13 people – 12 Brits and a Moroccan – were arrested and hundreds of ecstasy tablets, heroin, baseball bats, knives and ammunition similar to that used in the shoot-out were recovered from the suspects' homes.

An Ibiza police source said at the time: 'We fear a return to gun violence. We have been lucky so far this year that there have been no gunfights. But we fear it is only a matter of time.' A couple from Liverpool were also later arrested in Ibiza accused of being part of the British drugs gang behind that same gun battle.

West London drug dealer Jazzy warns that Ibiza's days as a number one destination for clubbers are numbered if the evil drug barons get a stranglehold on the island. 'These big British gangs are ruining everything. They've made the streets unsafe and people will just stop going there eventually. The place will collapse. The thing is that Ibiza is all about drug taking, so if the police clean it up then that will kill it off, too.'

Jazzy believes the gang who shot the Liverpool gangsters were sending out a chilling message to their rivals. 'It made me think twice about going back there next summer. It's getting too dangerous and the price of drugs is also dropping, which means I'm making less profit. It's not worth the risk. If I was having a nice time with my mates and making a few bob on the side I'd probably just shrug my shoulders, but it's getting dangerous out there.'

Jazzy says the Liverpool gangs are the ones who seem intent on taking over the island. 'The Scousers are a scary lot. They seem very different from the rest of us. I don't need all this aggro. Think I'll go somewhere nice and quiet next summer. Kick back and not bother with all this shit. It ain't worth the risk.'

Back in the summer of 2004, Ibiza's famed dance-till-dawn clubs faced their first drought of the drugs that fuel them after the Spanish police launched 'Operation Garage' and ended up making their biggest ever seizure of the basic ingredient in ecstasy. The raw material for at least 200,000 ecstasy tablets was uncovered en route from the Netherlands as the island filled up for the summer with clubbers from Britain and the rest of Europe. Nine kilos of almost pure MDMA, the basic chemical ingredient of ecstasy tablets, was found being prepared for shipment in a house on the outskirts of Madrid. A total of nine people from Spain, Italy, the Netherlands, Puerto Rico and the US were arrested during the operation.

A couple of weeks earlier, a dozen drug dealers selling ecstasy in the San Antonio district of Ibiza, the haunt of many young British visitors, were arrested after police installed closed-circuit television cameras outside clubs. But the reality is that such operations make only a small dent on the lucrative drugs trade during the peak summer months.

Ibiza clubs such as Privilege (earlier known as Ku), described as 'the world's biggest club', Amnesia, Es Paradis, Eden, Pacha and Space attract tens of thousands of young British clubbers during the summer, often with special nights hosted by British DJs. Drugs are formally banned by most clubs but ecstasy is still considered to be the Ibiza clubber's favourite recreational aid, even though it is not allowed inside such premises.

The infamous Ku, renamed Privilege a couple of years ago, holds 7,000. It has a swimming pool, restaurant, shop, two dance floors and an outdoor terrace that resembles a full-scale botanical garden. Despite all that, the club often can't accommodate all its potential customers. After being taken over by club group Cream, people queued from 8pm for at least two hours just to get a cab there from the ever-popular British haunt of San Antonio.

Ibiza's vast drug scene was even linked to the 11 March 2004 train bombings in Madrid, which killed 191 people. The mainly Moroccan Islamist bombers who blew up four morning commuter trains financed their operations and the purchase of dynamite with drug money. One of them was Jamal Ahmidan, a known drug trafficker who blew himself up, together with a police officer and six other radical Islamists, when they were surrounded by the police a few weeks after the attacks. Ahmidan had travelled to Ibiza the week before the attacks, apparently to close a trafficking deal. One of his contacts in Ibiza was even arrested by the judge investigating the Madrid bombings.

The British magazine *Mixmag* – which is devoted to clubs and dance – even highlighted to its readers the way Ibiza has come under pressure from underworld gangs trying to cash in on the island's druggie reputation. 'If you take drugs in Ibiza this summer, you deserve to know what your money is paying for,' an article in the magazine said. 'More club tourists means more gangsters to supply their drugs, more drug-related crime and more clubbers going to jail than ever.'

Several years ago the British vice-consul on the island, Michael Birkett, resigned, claiming he was increasingly being forced to deal with British 'degenerates'. In many ways it seems that the only winners are the gangsters running the drugs across the island.

By the end of the summer of 2008, the gang wars that people like Jazzy had feared on Ibiza had broken out with a vengeance as British crime gangs teamed up with Spanish ETA members in a lucrative drugs business that killed eight on the island in the space of a few months.

Mobsters from Liverpool, London, Newcastle and Cardiff are buying huge slices of the multimillion pound Class-A drugs market from Basque separatists ETA. And they are flooding venues in the dance resort, raking in up to £6,000 a day from designer drugs as the battle for the brutal drug trade heats up. The violent clashes between the gangs are threatening to kill off for good the sun-kissed island's reputation as Europe's party capital.

One British underworld source claimed the Spanish terrorist group ETA was masterminding the Ibiza drugs market in order to raise cash for its operations on the Spanish mainland. ETA even 'contracted' their drug supply work to Spanish and UK gangs. Teams of middlemen on the island slice up 'patches' where the dealers are allowed to work peddling the drugs. But ETA's involvement is setting the gangsters up against each other. One dealer explained: 'There are more drugs than ever before in Ibiza because ETA is getting greedy and allowing many more people to deal and the dealers are so desperate to make a profit they are cutting the drugs with anything they can lay their hands on.'

One Ibiza 'expert' is Danny from east London. He claims to be on 'the edge' of the island's drug scene and told me, 'Scousers probably take the biggest slice but Geordies, cockneys and boys from Cardiff have muscled their way in over the years. Supplies of every drug you can find – but mainly ecstasy – are then sold to clubbers by runners they send from their home cities. They are usually kids who will do anything for a get-rich-quick lifestyle. And, let me tell you, it's some lifestyle. The big-hitters over here have the villas, the yachts, the drugs, the women, the guns and the glam. And they don't have to do much for it.'

Most dealers on the island boast that they have 'everything under the sun. Es, MDMA, coke, phet (speed), ket (ketamine), crack, GHB, weed.' One proudly said: 'This stuff is the bollocks. It'll all blow your head off.'

In the island's most down-market party town, San Antonio, ecstasy is still by far the biggest seller. Different strains of ecstasy are given designer names to increase their appeal to clubbers. Tablets called 'Louis Vuittons', 'Versaces', 'Apples' and 'Hearts' are just a few of the different sorts being sold. 'The kids tend to go for the names. They don't have a clue what's in them but if they sound good they'll do them,' one dealer explained.

But the chemicals being pumped into the drugs are lethal. At least half a dozen Brit holidaymakers are believed to have died from the after-effects of drug-taking on the island since 2007. One gangland source said, 'No one wants to see anyone killed but this is a multimillion pound industry and we don't force these kids to take drugs. It is their decision.

There are certainly times when Ibiza sounds like an island at war with itself.

EL NORTE

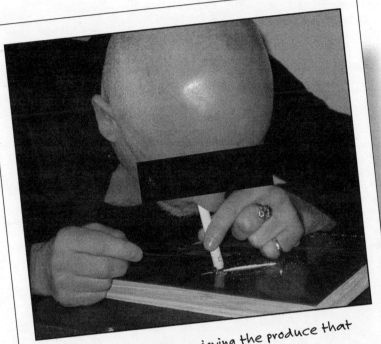

One British gangster enjoying the produce that nets him millions of pounds every year

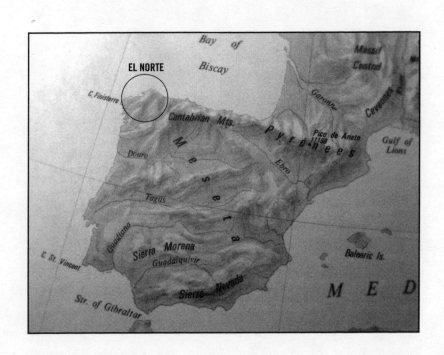

13

MOST OF THE drug 'activity' on the north coast of Spain is centred on the north-west province of Galicia, where shootings and the sudden disappearance of gangsters is commonplace. No wonder then that it's known as 'The Coast of Death'. It's like a lawless territory straight out of the Wild West – a corner of Spain that has been virtually left to run itself, with chilling results. In Galicia many gangsters have been sent to the bottom of the sea by their rivals. The Galician smugglers specialise in transporting vast shipments of cocaine from sea to land. They take a 30 per cent cut before handing it on to the criminal gangs for distribution around Europe.

And it is Galicia which has helped turn Spain into the biggest point of entry for cocaine in Europe. That has brought phenomenal wealth to what was the country's poorest region. The numerous coves and beaches of the *rias* – estuaries – make perfect landing places. Boats known as *planeadoras*, commonly used by local mussel farmers, make contact with bigger vessels out at sea at night.

The movement of drugs in Galicia is controlled by a number of well-established local families but a couple of hard-nosed British gangs have muscled into the area in recent years. That's where Sammy, from Leeds, comes in. His survival in this deadly corner of the north-west tip of Spain is a miracle in itself. It's a desolate area dominated by the mega-wealthy, cold-blooded Spanish traffickers – many of whom are ex-fishermen – and South American criminals.

Sammy met me during one of his rare trips south to the Costa del Sol, where I was introduced to him by a drug baron called Chet. Sammy's career as a reckless young armed robber on the streets of Manchester had landed him with a long stretch in the notorious Whitemoor prison back in the early 1990s. 'When I finished my probation I took the first flight here,' he told me. 'I'd met this Spanish drug dealer inside who told me that Galicia was the place to be, not the Costa bloody Sol where all the Flash Harrys are shooting each other and treading on each other's toes. This is where the stuff comes in. This is the real place to be if you want to earn big money out of drugs.'

Sammy likes to make everything sound very easy but in reality he had to work extremely hard to get a toehold in the Galician drugs scene. 'Brits like me stick out like a sore thumb up here. The Latins don't like northern Europeans and when I first turned up most of them thought I was an undercover copper.' But, explained Sammy, this actually worked to his advantage. 'You see, no one tried to have a pop at me like they would have if they'd just thought I was some villain from Manchester, which is what I am. They all left me alone and that gave me time to start building up contacts.'

And 'contacts' are the key to getting anywhere when it

comes to the drugs market in Galicia. Sammy continued: 'I sold myself to the heavy boys here by explaining that I had good connections back in the UK and in all the Spanish resorts popular with the Brits. They were using middlemen to handle the sales of cocaine. But when I came along they realised they could supply it direct to me.'

Sammy now runs a gang of six other Brits and lives in a quiet village inland from the main coastal drop-off points for the mass of cocaine that is brought in by fishing boats every week here. But Sammy and his men have had a lot of close shaves along the way. He explained: 'The Spanish and the South Americans round here are as hard as nails. They shoot first and ask questions later and one time about a hundred grand's worth of coke went missing from a shipment I picked up on a beach. But when I went back to the local guy responsible for the delivery he pulled a gun on me for daring to suggest he'd stolen the produce.

'It turned out that he was worried that if word got back to his bosses, he'd be made an example of and literally left to hang out to dry. Then a few days later this bloke and five of his mates burst into my house and tied up my wife and kid and then found me in a bar in a nearby village and demanded that I retract all my accusations or he'd have my kid's throat slit. It was heavy stuff because where I come from you never involve the family of a criminal, but round here all those rules mean jack shit.'

However Sammy eventually 'sorted out' that situation in his own inimitable style. 'I walked outside of that bar with those blokes and pulled an AK-47 out of the trunk of my motor and threatened to spray it around a bit so they'd have to do a very nimble tap dance. Then I told him to call his men off my family. He climbed down completely, my wife and kid were freed unharmed and from that moment on I had the utmost respect from all the gangsters in Galicia.'

These days, Sammy stays very much in the shadows while his gang deals directly day-to-day with the drug barons. His operation involves a van packed with 'produce', which is either driven south to the Costa del Sol or north up through France or Holland, then across the Channel and into the UK. Sammy reckons on splitting € 200,000 between himself and his small gang every month.

Sammy owns a luxuriously appointed farmhouse overlooking a stunning valley filled with pine trees, complete with swimming pool and two Dobermans. 'Life is good for me at the moment but I'm always on my guard. The characters that run all the cocaine coming in here by fishing boat from South America are fuckin' dangerous. I know only too well that they'd grass me up to get rid of me if they felt I was a risk. Other Brits and Paddies out here have paid that sort of price for upsetting the locals.'

By 2005, the Galician clans had stepped up their connections to the many British gangsters based in Spain. That's when law enforcement officials from Spain, Portugal and Britain launched joint operations to seize fishing vessels off the northern Spanish coast. Nearly five tons of cocaine was recovered in 2005. Dozens of people were arrested, including a number of British gangsters.

But their success came about because of one of the most sophisticated sting operations in criminal history. For when armed Spanish police confronted a ship called the *Atlantic Warner* off the Galician coast, they knew that almost all the crew were undercover British customs officials and members of the Portuguese navy. The boat itself was actually owned by HM Customs & Excise. Undercover British investigators had so thoroughly infiltrated the drug network that they not only knew a British gang was trying to smuggle cocaine into Europe, but were able to offer a vessel for the transportation of the drugs.

The real smugglers were a group of British criminals living on the Costa del Sol and they'd just delivered one of Europe's biggest cocaine hauls – with a street value of £225 million – into the hands of Customs.

When the Spanish police's elite special operations group boarded the *Atlantic Warner*, there had been only one actual genuine smuggler on board. He was the gang's 'notary', who was there to ensure that the 157 sacks of cocaine unloaded from a ship from Venezuela were then put aboard four boats off Spain's north-west coast. The British undercover team played their part so convincingly that they reportedly scuffled with a naval boarding party who ambushed their boat.

The cocaine on board had been bought from gangsters in Colombia's Norte del Valle, who'd transported it by river to Venezuela and, from there, loaded it on to a vessel near Isla

Margarita. That vessel then had a rendezvous with the *Atlantic Warner* and handed over the drugs.

The Galician clan known as Los Caneos, led by local godfather Daniel Baulo, had been due to send a team of speedboats to rendezvous with the *Atlantic Warner* off the coast of north-west Spain. The cocaine would then have been off-loaded at coves and beaches along Galicia's Atlantic coast. The Galicians were to keep a cut then hand the rest back to the original buyers so they could take it on to Britain and elsewhere.

Operation Tulle (Tulip), as British authorities dubbed it, was a lot different from other Spanish drug operations. It involved tailing the Los Caneos gang run by the notorious Baulo family. Journalists were never shown the *Atlantic Warner*, even after it was later taken to the Canary Island port of Las Palmas.

Witnesses later described the undercover British investigators as resembling extras from an advertisement for Fisherman's Friend sweets. The assault on the boat was stage-managed to appear genuine so that the *Atlantic Warner* might be used again in other operations.

Customs chiefs hoped to use the same tactic, and the same crew, again because the smugglers never realised that the boat that they had hired, the *Atlantic Warner*, was owned by HM Customs & Excise. The specially trained unit had earlier infiltrated the coastal area of Galicia. Some of the agents had been working there for years, mixing with underworld figures and shadowing British drugs barons.

Within days of the *Atlantic Warner* haul, a Spanish patrol vessel towed a yacht into the Galician port of El Ferrol. It had been boarded days after sailing from Trinidad under a German flag. On board was more cocaine destined for Britain. Some 230 kilos of the drug and £1 million in various currencies were recovered. One gangster was arrested in Britain and the mainly German network of smugglers was rounded up. The ringleader was a German living on the Costa del Sol where he had first made contact with British smugglers.

Eight more people including Brits, Spaniards and Colombians, were arrested as part of Operation Tulle in March 2006. Miguel García Izquierdo, director of a Spanish police unit specialising in drug trafficking and organised crime, revealed that the gang had the 'highest capacity ever seen for smuggling cocaine into Spain'. Local gang chief Daniel Baulo and his brother Carlos were among those arrested in Galicia.

Then in March 2006 Dubliners Timothy Kieran O'Toole and James Carabini were arrested in the Costa del Sol at the same time. Both men held dual Irish and British nationality. O'Toole was born in Dublin, but spent most of his life in Britain. Carabini was also born in Ireland's capital city and was well known to Irish police. The huge cocaine haul, which had been in transit from Colombia to Spain, was due for distribution to Ireland, the UK and other European countries. Also arrested at the same time was a British man, Ian Stephen Davenport. All three were living in Spain.

Over the years the two main smuggling gangs, the Charlins and Los Caneos, had earned hundreds of millions of pounds but, as with any business, the gangs knew they needed to find new markets if they were to survive.

Manuel Charlin had worked hand-in-hand with Manuel Baulo – father of gang-leader-in-waiting Daniel Baulo – and founder of the Los Caneos gang. In 1989 Charlin senior was sent to prison and asked Manuel Baulo to travel to Mexico on his behalf to oversee his next smuggling venture. Baulo travelled with Charlin's 28-year-old daughter, Josefa, and several other members of his associate's gang and successfully smuggled six tons of cocaine into Galicia.

A few years later, Baulo and Charlin fell out and the two gangs fought a series of bloody battles, which saw many killed, including Baulo's nephew. In early 1994, Manuel Baulo was arrested by the Spanish authorities and agreed to give evidence against Charlin.

When Charlin's daughter Josefa heard of this, she telephoned Baulo's wife and told her, 'You know what happened to your nephew? Well, the same thing is going to happen to you.' Josefa then arranged for a Colombian hitman to travel to Galicia. He later claimed she paid him £100,000 in cash and handed him the weapons with which to do the job. A few days later Manuel Baulo was shot dead. His wife, who was with him at the time, has been confined to a wheelchair ever since.

After the killing, Josefa Charlin went on the run, even though she had taken over leadership of the gang in 1998.

She once famously used her own daughter to launder drug money, passing more than £2 million through the child's account. Josefa Charlin even hired another Colombian gunman, Hernando Gomez, and his two henchmen to kill rival Carmina Carballo and her husband. Gomez and his colleagues – experienced *sicarios* hardened by Colombia's cocaine wars – went straight to Carmina's house in the Galician fishing village of Cambados and unleashed a hail of bullets. Unfortunately for Josefa, the hit went wrong and the husband was killed, but Carmina survived – although she also ended up in a wheelchair.

Living under the false identity of Angela Acha, Josefa kept one step ahead of the authorities – and the Baulo gang – until December 2006 when, at the age of 49, she was caught and sentenced to 17 years for drugs offences. In court she claimed that the Baulo family were the only ones involved in trafficking and that she was innocent.

Both Carmina and Josefa represented a new, sinister breed of female Galician cocaine 'capos' whom British and other foreign gangs in Spain have had to deal with in order to get a slice of the lucrative shipments that arrive on this deserted coastline from across the Atlantic in South America. Galicia's peasant women had long taken pride in their role as strong-willed matriarchs with absolute power over house, farm and family. In the old days their fishermen husbands were always away at sea braving the waters around what is known locally as 'The Coast of Death'.

A classic example of these riches is the palatial Pazo de

Baifin, an imposing country mansion surrounded by 35 acres of trellised vines bearing the special grapes that produce the sharp, young white wines of Rias Baixas. This imposing turn-of-the-century mansion replete with coats of arms, square turrets and battlements, is famous in Spain, but not for its wine. For this was once the home of another celebrated Galician female drug 'capo' called Esther Lago.

Lago is currently locked up in jail so visitors who call on the videophone at the entrance gate to this vast mansion are no longer frightened away by her heavies. It is an exquisite house built 100 years ago and styled after a French chateau, with spacious rooms, ornate, carved wooden ceilings and intricately laid parquet floors.

Lago's arrest came as police began to crack down on Galicia's *narcos* a couple of years ago. Not surprisingly, there is a wall of silence surrounding the drug gangs. Their wealth has pumped hundreds of millions of euros into the region. Fear and admiration prevents locals tipping police off, even though everybody knows who the drug gangsters are.

In the port city of Vigo, a group of mainly middle-class mothers whose children have succumbed to cocaine and other addictions have made the narcos' lives as difficult as possible. They even tried to tear down the iron gates of Lago's Pazo de Baion and chased hit 'victim' Carmina Carballo down the street in her wheelchair after she appeared in court. These ferocious middle-class mums, attired in fur coats, twinsets and angora sweaters, say their main aim has been to break the silence that surrounds the drug mafias.

In 2005, a British man with connections in Galicia was arrested in yet another international operation on the Costa del Sol. He was alleged by authorities to be the mastermind behind a gang and was charged with drug trafficking and money laundering. That same Brit had direct links going back to the founder of the Charlins gang, crime lord Manuel Charlin. And the increasingly close relationship between British gangsters and Galicia's drug dealers continues to provoke more battles between gangs, especially those from Colombia, renowned for their extreme violence, and who are extremely pissed off that the Brits have invaded their 'turf'.

Colombian Orlando Sabogal Zuluaga – one of Galicia's most deadly residents who also happened to have been, at the time of his arrest, one of the world's most wanted and violent drugs traffickers – was finally arrested in November 2006, in the Madrid commuter town of Majadahonda. His arrest came as part of a global crackdown on the violent Colombian Norte del Valle cartel and its offshoots, which were thought to be responsible for some 1,000 murders related to the drug trade.

Sabogal was one of a group of four Colombians who took over the reins of the country's biggest drug-trafficking outfit after the arrest and deportation to the United States of drug baron Luis Hernando Gómez Bustamante in 2004. Sabogal was known as 'Alberto' or 'The Monkey' amongst his peers, and few dared take him on because of his reputation as a complete 'loose cannon'.

The US state department offered a $5 million reward for information leading to Sabogal's arrest, but have always refused to say whether anyone was actually given that reward money.

The Norte del Valle cartel, based in the Cauca valley and the south west of Colombia, has become the country's most notorious group. Another Norte del Valle leader called Diego León Montoya Sánchez remains on the FBI's ten most-wanted list to this day, alongside Osama bin Laden.

The Colombians based in Galicia are renowned as the masters when it comes to laundering the proceeds of drugs. Their gangs operate through corrupt bureau de changes, couriers and complex electronic money transfers between accounts.

These vast sums – £50 million is known to have been laundered in Spain over a three-year period (2001–2004) and returned to the notorious Cali cartel in Colombia – prove beyond doubt that vast fortunes can be made.

When one Colombian gang member was arrested in Galicia with €1million in cash he was soon crying his eyes out. But that was because he was worried about how he was going to repay the seized money to the cartels. He knew only too well that if the cartels didn't get their cash he was a dead man.

In February 2006, two black Mercedes hearses drove slowly through the fishing town of Cambados in Galicia with huge wreaths pinned to their sides as mourners walked the familiar path to the cemetery to place two more cocaine war victims in their graves. The mothers of the victims trailed behind. The press stood at a respectful, frightened distance as the bodies of Ricardo Feijóo, 35, and his cousin, Angel, 25, were carried off to the hillside graveyard alongside the 15th-century ruins of the Santa Marina church.

Their charred corpses had been discovered two months earlier at an abandoned mill-house down a track a few miles from Cambados, the latest victims of the vicious cocaine wars being fought in Galicia. 'They kidnapped (the victims), they interrogated them, they tortured them and then they killed them,' said local police commissioner Jaime Iglesias, head of a police unit dealing with the increasingly violent drug gangs of this part of Galicia.

The two Feijóo cousins had been kidnapped in front of one of their wives by men who did not bother to hide their faces. A week earlier their warehouse, which contained a 14-metre speedboat equipped with two 300hp engines, had been burnt out. The boat, which was capable of outrunning police launches, would have been used for a rendezvous off the coast with the trawlers or container ships that bring the drugs across the Atlantic from Latin America or pick them up at one of the numerous clearing houses now operating in west Africa.

At the home of Ricardo Feijóo, near the River Umia in Barrantes, the family was no stranger to tragedy. The body of his brother had been washed up on the Canary Islands just over a year earlier. And another brother died as his speedboat crashed charging through a Galicia sea loch. Meanwhile, the killers of the two cousins were believed to have slipped across the border with Portugal after the double slaying, then burnt their car and disappeared.

A white sheet hung from the handsome belltower of the stone San Francisco church where the funeral mass for the two cousins was held. The parish priest, José Aldao, hung it up there as part of a wider protest throughout the district, aimed at urging rebellion against the grip that cocaine smuggling has on parts of the local economy, and on the imagination of young people looking for quick, easy money.

The death of the Feijóo cousins followed that of Ramón Outeda, shot in daylight as he opened his front door in the same fishing village of Cambados. Three other local traffickers were found shot in different parts of Galicia in 2005. Another was kidnapped and is presumed dead. The killers are 'normally Latin Americans or others who live in Madrid or abroad, especially Colombians,' said one local law enforcement officer who had an intimate knowledge of the drug smugglers of Galicia.

It seems that these days occasional police victories over the traditional Galician smuggling families have left a void that is being filled by young, hot-blooded traffickers who settle scores in a vicious manner. 'The new generation is a lot more violent and soulless ... they have different values from the old patriarchs,' added the local law enforcement officer.

With the older generation of Galician smugglers often

struggling to control their empires from jail cells, a myriad of small groups offer services for smuggling cocaine on to isolated beaches in Galicia and, from there, across Europe.

Fear of being killed by the gangsters keeps many local people from cooperating with police and stops others raising their voices in protest against the new traffickers. Press photographers are regularly beaten up at events such as funerals and weddings of the drug lords.

Also in 2006, five Britons were arrested after a British-registered boat carrying eight tons of cannabis, worth £24 million, was seized off the Galician coast. The fishing vessel was believed to have left Britain some weeks earlier, docked in Galicia, and then headed towards Morocco. It was boarded during its return journey. That same year, Spanish police broke up a drug-trafficking and money-laundering ring, seizing cash and property worth more than £8 million. A Moroccan-born man with British citizenship, his British wife and a Spaniard were among those arrested.

By the middle of this decade Spain was accounting for 60 per cent of the drug seizures by police in Europe. This put Spain third in the world ranking for cocaine finds – behind Colombia and the US. An average of more than 50 tons a year has been seized by Spanish police in recent years. But, even with the latest round of seizures, Spanish customs officials believe they stop less than 10 per cent of the drug traffic into Galicia. At least five tons get through every month. Previous attempts at dismantling the smuggling networks have ultimately done little more than change the names and faces at the head of the organisations.

There are also questions about the effectiveness of the Spanish judicial system when it comes to dealing with its biggest offenders. In January 2002, Carlos Ruiz Santamaría, alias 'El Negro' and accused of being the head of one of Spain's biggest drug gangs, was charged in connection with the smuggling of 11 tons of cocaine. While he was on remand awaiting trial, the psychiatrist at Madrid's Valdemoro prison judged Ruiz to have extreme depression and said there was a risk he might commit suicide. He had lost 15kg in prison and suffered wild mood swings. The judges ignored the protests of the prosecution, who said his alleged depression could be treated in a prison hospital, and released him. The prosecution had demanded a sentence of 60 years and a fine of around £280 million. Despite this, he was released on bail of just £18,000 on condition that he regularly reported to police. He has not been seen since and is believed to have returned to his native Colombia.

By the beginning of 2007, the success of certain undercover police operations had at least put enough pressure on the drug gangs to make them begin switching some smuggling operations from the Galicia region to southern Spain. One British former drugs baron now on the run from Spanish authorities told me that some Moroccan hashish gangs were taking over from Galicians as cocaine traffickers. 'The operation when the British customs men ran that fake ship definitely had a bad effect on the cocaine running out of Galicia,' he said.

But other gangs claimed it made little difference and that the Galicians were pretending to switch their operations just to make the authorities believe they had succeeded. However, it was certainly true that the Colombian cartels were not so keen to risk sending a ship loaded with narcotics directly to offload onto smaller vessels close to Galicia or the Canary Islands. They became increasingly convinced it was much safer to enter West African ports such as Guinea-Conakry, Guinea-Bissau, and those in Ghana, Togo and Sierra Leone. These seaports were badly policed and the criminals could even leave their produce 'sleeping' for long periods of time.

Then the cocaine shipments were moved up to Morocco where they would be transported by the highly experienced local hashish smugglers on semirigid launches, capable of 45 knots.

In January 2009, the Colombians sent out a chilling message to their enemies when a 'traitor' drug baron was shot dead in a Madrid hospital by a hitman. The shooter entered the room of leading Colombian drug lord Leonidas Vargas, 59, took out a pistol with a silencer attached and pumped four bullets into his victim, killing him instantly.

On the so-called 'Coast of Death', drugs continue to dominate the landscape. Huge seaside mansions belonging to the mega-wealthy 'capos' prove that the smuggling traditions, which have dominated this area for more than 200 years, continue to make this coastline the most criminally lucrative in Europe.

COSTA BRAVA

A back room in one of the most notorious clubs on the Costa Brava

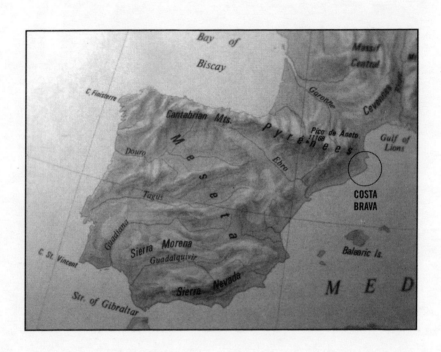

14

THE NORTH-EASTERN coastline of Spain – known as the Costa Brava – is not as popular with Brits as the Costa del Sol and Costa Blanca further south but it is renowned for having a more sophisticated criminal element. As one veteran British gangster called Alec told me, 'It's much classier up here. This is where the serious chaps operate.' And the famous city of Barcelona is undoubtedly at the hub of the up-market gang war which has blighted this area for so many years. Huge numbers of so-called 'sex slave' women 'imported' from eastern Europe and South America into Spain's vice trade are brought through Barcelona en route to their final destination in brothels across the nation, and many of the drugs brought from Africa in the south also travel a similar path.

Elena is a half-Spanish, half-English woman in her mid-forties who describes herself as a 'mummy' to many of the young women brought through Barcelona. She openly admits 'training' the women as dungeon queens and submissives as well as for other sexual practices. Elena is paid by a Romanian gang who specialise in smuggling the women into Spain, and although she likes to look upon herself as their 'mummy' or guardian, she is effectively sanctioning the most twisted aspects of this sick trade.

However, I put my misgivings about Elena to one side so that she would provide me with an insight into the secret trade in women, which as well as helping to line the pockets of many British and foreign gangsters has sparked a mini-war all of its own in Barcelona. Elena explained: 'The Romanians guard their women as if they are shipments of drugs. I try to explain to the girls what is expected of them and how they need to learn to cut out their emotions when possible. But it's hard for them, although I tell them that if they look on it as only a job then they will cope fine.'

Elena says that in the last couple of years UK-based gangs have started importing girls into Spain from the UK. Ironically, many of these girls are originally from eastern bloc countries; they have gone to the UK to find work in the first place and then they have been 'persuaded' to work as prostitutes.

Elena revealed that two British gangs in particular have gained a fearsome reputation in recent years. 'They are nearly all young guys, under 30, and they act more like the eastern Europeans than the old traditional criminals from the UK, which means they're deadly. I heard that one of them has killed at least three other gangsters since they arrived in Barcelona.'

Elena admits she was once a prostitute herself but insists she is sympathetic to the women. She said that the prospective prostitutes are all kept at a safe house in the suburbs of Barcelona before being shipped out to many of the hundreds of roadside brothels that line Spain's main routes. 'One of the Romanians I work for told me recently that each girl can help earn them more than € 50,000 over a two-year period working in the brothels. We are talking about hundreds of girls each year so that is a lot of money.'

The girls themselves are 'shuttled' from brothel to brothel every few weeks in order to prevent them being spotted by the authorities, who are constantly checking the clubs for work papers. 'One week a girl could be in Málaga in the south and then she is moved up to Vigo in the north. They do this deliberately to make sure they are not caught by the police,' Elena pointed out.

Many of the girls 'imported' from the UK have worked in massage parlours back in Britain after being forced into the UK from their eastern European or South American homes in the first place. 'This is where the British gangs are causing so many problems because they are 'stealing' these girls from their original pimps and then forcing them over here to Barcelona,' explained Elena.

Elena says that only a few months previously a gang of Albanian pimps arrived in Barcelona with the express intention of tracking down half a dozen girls who had worked for them back in London before a British gang persuaded them to travel to Spain. 'I heard the Albanians were out to kill the Brits if they found them. They considered the girls to be their property and were outraged that they were 'stolen' right under their noses in London.'

Elena goes on to say that the Albanian gang toured dozens of brothels in the area looking for the girls but eventually gave up and went back to London. 'These guys were very scary and I know many of the girls were better off in Spain working for the Brits, because they are nicer to them than the Albanians.'

But Elena believes the gang wars among the vice dealers in Barcelona will get a lot worse. 'They're going to get more and more violent as they get increasingly desperate. The other problem is that drugs have dropped so much in price that more and more of these gangs are wanting a piece of the sex trade.'

Elena explains she is trying to save enough money to leave Barcelona and head back to her family in the UK. She already sends back £500 a month to her mother who looks after her 17-year-old son. 'All I really care about is my family. My son wants to go to university and I intend to pay for all that so that he can get the sort of chances I never got. Meanwhile, I'm just trying to keep a low profile here, although its not easy. Once I have enough saved up I am going to retire and go back to England. I want a normal life.'

A fugitive drugs gangster was brought back to Britain in October 2002 to serve a 22-year jail sentence after police traced him to the Costa Brava. John Barber, 36, from Bolton, was arrested in the picturesque fishing village of Sant Pol de Mar, just north of Barcelona. Barber disappeared with his lawyer's-clerk girlfriend Victoria Dudson, 22, from Stretford, near Manchester halfway through a trial at Liverpool Crown Court, where he was accused of conspiracy to supply millions of pounds worth of Class-A drugs. His girlfriend worked for his defence solicitors and was reported to have been pregnant at the time. It was said in court that when police raided Barber's property they recovered 15 kilos of hashish worth £45,000, three luxury cars, two imitation guns, false car numberplates and £4,000 worth of euros.

Barber – a member of a gang based in Bolton, Lancashire – was sentenced in his absence to 22 years. The same UK gang was thought by police to be behind the murder of five-year-old Dillon Hull in Bolton in 1997. The boy was shot by a bungling gunman sent by the gang leader who was aiming for the boy's father, John Bates. That particular gang leader was himself gunned down by a criminal rival in the town of Wigan.

In November 2008, another Costa-Brava based Brit was held on suspicion of shooting one man dead and badly wounding another. Civil engineer Darren Coupland, 41, was arrested over claims he killed a German and shot another man in a row about a drug debt. Both men were found bleeding and close to death outside Coupland's villa near Barcelona.

The married father-of-two from Southend in Essex was stabbed in the throat during the clash and was taken to hospital following the incident, before being arrested.

In November 2007 Spanish police broke up a gang of mostly Romanians who were producing thousands of fake credit cards and using them to buy goods or obtain cash. A total of 44 people were arrested in the operation in the eastern provinces of Castellon and Tarragona on the Costa Brava.

Officers staged 23 raids and discovered six workshops where the credit cards were being produced. Around 2,000 fake cards were seized. The gang used contacts in Europe and North America to obtain stolen credit card numbers. The fake cards were used to buy goods in shops or on the Internet that were then sold, or to withdraw cash from bank dispensers. The head of the gang was among those arrested, but police would only say the network was made up 'largely' of Romanians.

Barcelona's reputation as home to many of the really big criminal fish is perfectly illustrated by Oded Tuito. He was a global pill-pushing gangster, whose Israeli Mafia team was the biggest operator in a booming international trade in the lucrative 'hug drug' ecstasy. But in May 2001 Tuito, who allegedly stamped his ecstasy pills with the Star of David and the Tweety Bird cartoon character that reminded him of his own name, was arrested in the coastal town of Castelldefels just outside Barcelona. His arrest provoked a deluge of extradition requests and police inquiries from four continents.

Tuito, 40, had half a dozen homes and as many aliases. In Spain he called himself Adel Tonitou and lived in a luxury Barcelona hotel. He kept his wife and family in France but travelled the world, directing his operations on the move. His base in Spain was well away from his main production and distribution bases, allowing him greater security. And even after Tuito's arrest, he continued directing shipments from his cell in Madrid's Soto del Real prison until a global police operation against the rest of his gang began in August 2001.

Three dozen of his alleged associates, part of an organisation that shipped several million pills a year, were eventually arrested in Spain and as far away as Los Angeles and Melbourne, Australia. Tuito's principal lieutenants, Michael Elkaiam and Simon Itach, were also picked up in Barcelona. The gang was also alleged to have trafficked in cannabis and cocaine and was linked to a notorious firm of Israeli armed robbers who targeted jewellers' shops in Barcelona.

America's Drug Enforcement Agency had been about to put Tuito's name on its public list of the world's eight most-wanted drug-trafficking suspects. Tuito was eventually charged in New York, Los Angeles and Pittsburgh, and also connected to investigations in Florida, Kentucky and Delaware. On top of this he was wanted by the Israeli courts. Spanish police, meanwhile, were investigating allegations that he also trafficked ecstasy to the island of Ibiza.

The Israeli allegedly made a fortune out of exploiting the mark-up on a pill that cost him only 30p to make. 'He was buying pills for 50 cents apiece in Holland and selling them here for $28 (£19). That's quite a mark-up,' said one DEA agent in New York.

Tuito bought up the entire production of pills from several clandestine laboratories in the Netherlands, which were driven overland to Spain, Belgium, France and Germany. A variety of courier services were then used to sneak the drugs out of the EU. Strippers from New York, Spanish teenagers and even pensioners took the drugs to the US, Canada, Israel and Australia. Sometimes pills were packed into picture frames and sent via ordinary international messenger services. Tuito's gang also allegedly 'exported' to Latin America via Panama, and Asia via Thailand.

The arrival of Tuito highlighted a disturbing emergence in recent years of the Israeli Mafia. Interpol officials spotted their involvement with what was at that time considered the world's most popular illicit drug, with an estimated annual global consumption of more than 500 million pills.

In September 2005 the crack Spanish anti-crime police unit Unidad Contra redes de Inmigración y Falsificación Documental (UCRIF) in Barcelona rounded up a bunch of suspected gang members in a swoop on the Chinese district of Trafalgar. Nine alleged members of Triads were indicted on charges of threatening and extorting money from local Chinese merchants.

Spanish-based Chinese gangs such as Red Sun – which is also active in France and Italy – are among the most powerful of all the criminal gangs of different nationalities that thrive in Spain. They specialise in manufacturing and supplying amphetamines and other synthetic drugs. The gangs have sprung up in Barcelona due to the influx of Chinese immigrants from Fujian and Zhejiang, who have settled in both the suburbs and the city centre, where clothing stores flourish.

Ironically, it's always the Chinese community who are the first to suffer from the presence of Triad organised crime gangs in their midst. Early this year, a deadly duel with swords in a Chinese restaurant in Barcelona prompted the police to seriously consider setting up a special unit trained to fight organised Asian crime. The Barcelona police were more accustomed to battling against Latin American mobs or radical Islamic movements. Up until then it had relied on the Guardia Civil's intelligence centre in Madrid to centralise data concerning foreign gangs or movements. In addition to Madrid and Barcelona, the two Mediterranean cities of Valencia and Alicante, have become haunts of the Chinese gangs.

The Triads are the ones who seem to really scare the British and other foreign gangs in Spain. The Chinese Mafia works only within its own tight infrastructure and as such it makes it almost impenetrable to outsiders. Often their criminal enterprises are far more cold-blooded. Police in both Barcelona and Madrid have in recent years raided Triad-run brothels and rescued Chinese females, some of whom appeared to be under the age of 15 and had been specifically 'imported' from China in order to satisfy the demands of the brothels' Chinese immigrant customers.

One girl called Ms Ye who was rescued in Madrid in April 2007 told investigators she'd been forced to work in cramped conditions and cater for men who fantasised about having sex with children. It's reckoned that brothels run by Triad bosses in Spain make tens of millions of euros each year out of the sex trade.

Women usually get just a fraction of the money they are paid for their sexual services – the rest goes towards paying off their 'debt'. Spanish investigators cracked one Triad gang after a neighbour living next to one of the Triad brothels claimed children were being abused. When police arrived they thought many of the women were underage until they checked their passports and found they were aged between 24 and 29.

In Madrid, a specialised police unit arrested 14 leaders of six gangs who were running about 100 mainland women in a tightly controlled series of brothels across the country. They kept one step ahead of the police for months by changing the brothels every few weeks, sometimes working in hotels or operating a 'home delivery' service where girls would visit clients' homes. Official figures put the number of mainland Chinese in Spain at 90,000, although there are thought to be double the number working in the country's 'black economy'.

In April 2007, 40 Russian women were freed from sex slavery in a special police operation on the Costa Brava. Most of the women were from St Petersburg and had been held captive under threat of physical violence. Seven people, including the gang leader – an Albanian national – were arrested and charged with human trafficking and organising a prostitution ring. The gang also included three Russians, one Kosovo Albanian, and one Armenian.

In October 2007, Spanish police broke up an organised crime gang, which brought young women from Russia to Spain and forced them to work as prostitutes on the Costa Blanca. The ring, led by a Uruguayan national, sent hundreds of young women from Russia to Spain, and gang members then raped them and forced them to use cocaine.

In December 2000, Spanish and French police detained eight suspects allegedly belonging to a daredevil gang of robbers believed to have committed some of Europe's most spectacular heists. In a joint operation, police arrested the eight in the north-eastern Spanish town of Sitges, near Barcelona, and in a southern Paris suburb.

The gang, described by Interpol as Europe's most dangerous robbers, was suspected of a slew of thefts, all planned like military manoeuvres and using heavy arms. The gang were linked to the 1999 robbery of $3.4 million in cash from an armoured car company at Málaga airport, plus a 1996 aviation robbery in which two armed men wearing masks robbed a jetliner on the runway in the southern France city of Perpignan. They were also connected to the hold-ups of armoured trucks in French cities such as Limoges and Créteil. The robbers even identified themselves with the same names as characters in the 1995 crime thriller *Heat*, which starred Robert De Niro as the head of a gang of high-tech thieves.

During a search of the suspects' homes, police seized 20 assault rifles, 20 handguns, 12 grenades, one grenade launcher, 1.5kg (3lb) of explosives, 100kg (220lb) of ammunition and a large stash of cash. It later emerged that the suspects lived on the Costa Brava in luxury villas and socialised with the rich and famous.

In 2006, up in Girona, just north of Barcelona, Spanish police claimed they prevented a large-scale bank robbery when they finally detained the fugitive leader of a French and Spanish crime gang at his house in north-east Catalonia.

Louis Carboni was believed to be the head of the Corso Clan criminal gang from France's Mediterranean island of Corsica. The gang specialised in drug trafficking and armed robbery and had been planning the massive heist of an unidentified bank when they were arrested.

Following Carboni's apprehension, six other members of the gang were detained on Corsica by the French authorities. The gang was blamed for a series of violent robberies, among them the September heist of a jewellery store in southern Spain, when gang members opened fire on police and got away with more than €6 million (£5.4 million) worth of jewellery.

The Corso Clan was also responsible for Carboni's June 2001 escape from a Corsican prison. In a Hollywood movie-style operation, two men hijacked a helicopter and forced the pilot to fly to the jail where they picked up their leader.

Spanish police had been tracking Carboni since the end of 2001 when French authorities located him in the north-eastern province of Girona. Police arrested him and his female companion when they stormed his house before dawn one Saturday. They found a semiautomatic weapon in the house and a loaded pistol on Carboni's bedside table.

In January 2003, Spanish police smashed Europe's largest music, film and computer software piracy gang, making 40 arrests connected to an operation estimated to be worth £400 million. Eleven properties in Barcelona and the Spanish capital of Madrid were raided. Two lorries were needed by police to take away pirate copies of CDs and DVDs estimated to be worth £1.5 million. Also seized were 346 CD-copying machines, used around the clock to produce a pirate copy every four minutes at a potential loss to the music and film industry of £600 million a year.

The highly sophisticated gang supplied fraudulent CDs and DVDs to vendors across the country, producing more than 60 million items for sale. The 40 detainees were charged with copyright infringement, while some were also suspected of illegal entry into Spain. Twenty-nine of those arrested were Chinese, nine were Senegalese and two were Spanish. The two gang leaders were both Chinese, one of whom was illegally in Spain and the other, who owned a computer store, was using it as a cover for the piracy trade.

The leaders rented a warehouse from where they would transport blank compact discs and other source material in a van to special apartments where they could be copied. The warehouse and the flats were locked from the outside by the gang leaders, even though there were other Chinese working inside day and night. Senegalese gang members were in charge of distributing the faked material to the vendors that swamp the beaches and resorts of all the Costas during every season.

By the summer of 2005, Barcelona's reputation as one of Europe's most popular tourist destinations was over-shadowing, but unwittingly encouraging, another type of gang war on the Costa Brava. More than 6,000 visitors a day arrive in the city from Britain and that makes it prime territory for street-crime gangs looking for potential victims. In 2004, the British Consulate in Barcelona had to provide 1,000 emergency passports for tourists – a tenth of the 10,000 issued by the Foreign Office worldwide. Most of them were stolen by carefully organised gangs of pickpockets and thieves.

Some gangs have even developed highly specialised skills. They pose with a map and pretend to be lost, then ask a tourist if they can help and while the tourist is looking at the map, they take something from a rucksack. Another scam is to pose as a gypsy and offer some roses. While the tourists are being charmed by the roses, the robbers go through the tourists' pockets. The classic one is to throw shaving cream on a tourist's jacket, then take them to McDonald's to help them clean up. The tourist takes this as local friendliness and doesn't notice that their wallet is being stolen as their new 'friend' cleans off the mess.

Often these gangs on the streets of Barcelona battle with each other over what 'territory' they are allowed to commit crimes within. The gangs are mostly from South America but they guard their turf very carefully. If another gang tries to commit a crime inside their territory, guns are usually drawn and in a couple of recent cases, shots have been fired. These gangs are making tens of thousands of euros every month from street crimes. They even have contacts to whom they can sell stolen passports – many of these and other documents can be quickly altered and then sold on to the highest bidder. Passports are much more valuable than drugs.

Authorities in Barcelona say that the largest proportion of gangsters in the city are Moroccans. But even more disturbing is that nearly two-thirds of all criminals jailed in Barcelona are foreigners. One senior police source said: 'Immigration is linked to the rise of professional gangs who did the same in their countries.'

Gangs target popular tourist spots. The narrow streets of Barrio Gótico where Picasso lived, El Born with its fashionable bars, and La Rambla, Barcelona's most colourful thoroughfare, are popular with gangs. Their other haunts include the Eixample area, which includes Gaudí's unfinished La Sagrada Familia cathedral, and Gràcia, home to hip restaurants, where the winding streets often prove perilous for a tourist faced with a thief armed with a knife.

Also, one must never forget the gangs run by the Basque separatist group ETA. A suspected Basque militant was arrested in France in 2001 after a gang stole a huge haul of dynamite and he was identified by a witness as being one of the robbers. Gregorio Vicario Setién was arrested at a police roadblock after a gang of between five and ten suspected members of the ETA separatist organisation stole 1.6 tons of explosives in the south-eastern French town of Grenoble.

Setién, 42, was armed with an automatic pistol, carrying

false identity papers and driving a car with false plates, police said. A map of a detailed route leading from the scene of the crime to the Basque country was also in the car.

Back in 1993–94, Vicario Setién had been a member of ETA's Barcelona cell, which Spanish authorities blamed for eight attacks – two of them fatal – in northern Spain. ETA, which is fighting for an independent Basque homeland, has been blamed for more than 30 killings since it broke a truce in December 1999. Many of the attacks are thought to have been carried out with explosives stolen in France in the 1999 raid.

In November 2006, police in Barcelona arrested nine suspected members of a British-run gang, including a retired Spanish police inspector. The gang was alleged to have dressed as police officers to swoop on drug dealers, confiscate their 'produce' then sell it on themselves. Among items seized during the operation were 12 firearms, 25 knives, aerosols, 24 kilograms of hash, 17 grams of coke plus more than £50,000 in cash and a handful of samurai-style swords.

So, the Costa Brava continues to ring to the sound of gunfire as the area's numerous British and foreign gangs battle it out for control of the streets.

THE CANARIES

John Palmer's million pound yacht, Brave Goose of Essex, is still staffed and ready to sail at a few hours' notice in Tenerife just in case the master gangster is freed from jail earlier then expected.

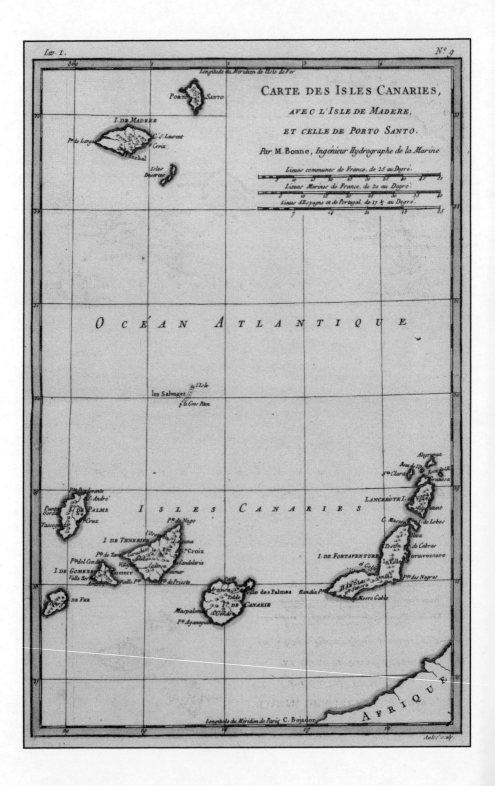

Longitude du Méridien de l'Isle de Fer

CARTE DES ISLES CANARIES,

AVEC L'ISLE DE MADERE,

ET CELLE DE PORTO SANTO.

Par M. Bonne, Ingénieur Hydrographe de la Marine

Lieues communes de France, de 25 au Degré.

Lieues Marines de France, de 20 au Degré.

Lieues d'Espagne et de Portugal, de 17 ½ au Degré.

OCÉAN ATLANTIQUE

les Salvages

ISLES CANARIES

AFRIQUE

Longitude du Méridien de Paris   C. Bojador

André sculp.

15

FOR MORE THAN 25 years, British tourists have been lured by the sun and sea of the famous Spanish colony, the Canary Islands, located just off the coast of north-west Africa. The most popular of these islands is Tenerife. On the surface and from a postcard it looks like a pleasant enough place. But there are pockets of British criminals here that have turned parts of the island into a sordid gangster's paradise.

No one place illustrates this point better than the tatty, run-down resort of Playa de las Américas, which is crammed with members of the lower end of British criminality. Many of the villains who operate here believe they can escape justice more easily because the Canary Islands are as far from the Spanish mainland as Spain itself is from the UK. As a result, they hide out among the innocent British tourists who flock to this resort all year round because of the sub-tropical climate.

I first came across Tommy Jackson when I was filming a TV documentary about some of the islands most notorious 'faces'. He has lived in Playa de las Américas for more than 15 years and freely admits that during that time he has dealt drugs, pimped women and pulled some outrageous scams. 'It's the only way to survive out here. This is a shithole really.

There's not much decent straight work around so you have to do whatever comes yer way,' explained Tommy.

The locals here in Playa de las Américas loathe the shirt-less, balding Brits who've turned their once picturesque community into a cesspit of criminality. They've undoubtedly brought with them an avalanche of villainy, which in turn has sparked much resentment between the locals and the scumbag Brits. One longtime resident told me, 'The British are filthy pigs. They have no respect for property or other people. They come here and drink and take drugs and then piss and vomit in the street. Many people here would like them all to leave so this island can go back to the peaceful place it once was.'

Even chirpy Tommy sympathises with the locals' plight.

'The Spanish are always happy when they hear about a Brit whose been gunned down or beaten up. It's one less pain in the arse for them to deal with. I don't blame them,' he says. 'Most of the Brits here are down-market duckers and divers who are so off their 'eads they wouldn't see a bullet coming their way if it was fired an inch from their faces. This is not a nice environment and we, the Brits, have made it like this.'

In some ways Playa de las Américas is like the Canary Islands' equivalent to one of the notorious crime-ridden *favelas* (slums) of Rio de Janeiro in Brazil. It's home to some of the poorest people on the island. Most of the gangsters here are small-time, 'wooden tops', not really capable of anything but the most blatant criminal behaviour. But behind the scenes are the so-called 'operators' who are constantly pulling the strings.

And, just like a Brazilian *favela,* many prying eyes greet strangers with deep suspicion when they step into Playa de las Américas. When I wandered into a British bar that was offering fish 'n' chips and one-euro pints of lager I was greeted with complete silence from half a dozen thickset guys with the obligatory hoop earrings and bald heads. When I asked the directions to another even more notorious criminals' bar, the Brit behind the bar literally ignored me. There was an undercurrent of violence in the air so I left without saying another word.

Tommy says that the gangsters who reign in this veritable no-man's-land, where the police just don't bother to tread very often, divide the resort up into specific areas. 'There are about half a dozen what I would call 'heavyweight Brit' gangs who run most of the big stuff here.' By 'big stuff' Tommy means cocaine and ecstasy and timeshare scams. 'These characters are pretty nasty and they'll have you done if you wind 'em up.'

Tommy continued: 'Its true there is a feeling out here that you can get away with just about anything because we are so far from the Spanish mainland. It's that attitude which has helped the gangsters continue to grow in strength. Round here everyone knows who the players are and we just make sure we don't cross them.'

As I strolled along the twisting pathway that runs along the promenade of Playa de las Américas it became even more clear that the Brits were running things in this part of town. Virtually every bar seemed to have a number of red-faced soccer-hooligan types wearing the St George's Cross T-shirts, swigging beers and whispering conspiratorially while watching the faces of everyone walking past. Many of the buildings looked as if someone had forgotten to finish them off with a proper lick of paint. When I went into a second bar to ask directions, the barman, a Midlander called Terry, asked me in a friendly manner what I was doing on the island. When I replied, he laughed nervously.

'You don't want to go round telling too many people what you're up to, mate, otherwise you might get a visit from one of those muppets,' he said, nodding towards a group of four pumped-up bulldog men with thick necks, sitting round a table outside. 'See that one with the sunglasses on?' Terry said, nodding straight at a man who looked like he had just come off the set of soccer hooligan film *The Football Factory*. 'His name is Gordon and he runs everything round here from the drugs to the women to the scams. Everyone has to pay him a chunk; otherwise they get a visit from Gordon's boys. He's a law unto himself. We even pay him a bit of protection money to make sure the bar doesn't burn down and or get smashed up.'

The beachfront at Playa de las Américas seemed to be buzzing with activity but the moment I stepped back just one block from the glittering, gaudy strip it all went rapidly downhill. As darkness fell, lots of neon lights flashed on and off and there seemed to be endless fast-food joints and tawdry souvenir shops but little else, apart from drunken Brits literally falling out of hole-in-the-wall bars.

Shoot-outs between British and foreign gangsters here on Tenerife are commonplace and within 24 hours of arriving on the island it became clear that one Brit above everyone else had used and abused this place in a truly extraordinary manner; he even had a notorious nickname – 'Goldfinger' – earned from his connections in the 1980s. John Palmer ran his £350 million timeshare empire just a stone's throw from Playa de las Américas. He had a dozen vintage cars parked in an underground car park just nearby, according to barman Terry. 'There's an old Merc in there that they say is 200K alone,' said Terry, his eyes virtually lighting up with the excitement of just mentioning Palmer's name. Later I saw those cars for myself and they were, indeed, an impressive collection.

Terry continued: 'It doesn't matter that Palmer's locked up again. He's the undisputed king of Tenerife. He's richer than the local government here. He's got lawyers, coppers, customs men, you name it. They're all in his pocket.'

No wonder in 2007 Palmer decided to return to Tenerife after serving half of an eight-year sentence in the UK for timeshare fraud. Trouble was, the Spanish authorities were feeling so humiliated by Palmer's money-making scams over the previous 20 years that they were determined to bring him to justice. Palmer's flight from London landed at the Reina Sofia Airport on Tenerife on a Tuesday afternoon in July 2007. The airport is close to the holiday resorts where a series of multimillion-pound timeshare scams had helped to turn Palmer into one of Britain's richest people.

Among the fellow passengers watching the 57-year-old

gather up his bags and prepare to disembark, however, were Spanish police officers who had been tracking him from Britain. He was about to be arrested once again. Grabbed by police shortly after leaving the plane, Palmer was immediately taken to a local police station before being transferred to Madrid to face the country's most celebrated investigating magistrate, Judge Baltasar Garzón.

Palmer had been imprisoned in the UK for defrauding 17,000 timeshare clients before getting out of jail two years early. But the charges he faced in Spain were potentially far more serious. The Spanish authorities alleged his gang had carried out 'multiple criminal activities' including 'timeshare fraud, money laundering, credit card fraud, threats, crimes against people's physical integrity and freedom, trafficking drugs, falsifying passports and possession of weapons.'

Spanish authorities also alleged that Palmer had continued to run a criminal empire while serving time in a British prison. Police estimated Palmer's timeshare and property empire in the Canary Islands, built up after he moved to Spain in 1985, to be worth at least £300 million. They estimated his overall wealth to be at least half a billion pounds, even with the global recession biting into this crooked tycoon's business investments.

Palmer's rearrest focused attention on the criminal underworld on Tenerife, which had been worrying the Spanish for many years. In the Spanish capital of Madrid, authorities openly admitted they were trying to crack down on the gangs who'd given the island a bad name. When

Palmer was earlier locked up in the UK, timeshare frauds continued in the hands of other people and vicious turf wars between gangs were commonplace. There were also numerous claims that local police officers and politicians were on the gangs' payrolls.

Back in January 2006 two former Palmer employees, Billy and Flo Robinson, were tortured and murdered on the island. Mrs Robinson was found in a pool of blood beside her silver Mercedes. Her husband's body was on the back seat of his Porsche. These sort of cold-blooded killings seem to have spurred the Spanish authorities into action. Nobody is pointing the finger directly at Palmer but there is no denying that Billy and Flo had crossed someone and paid for that with their lives.

Back in the mid-1980s, Palmer first came to public notice when it was alleged he helped to melt down gold stolen during the notorious £27 million Brinks-Mat robbery, in an oven in the garden of his home, near Bath in Somerset. But a jury cleared him of wrongdoing, and of laundering the 6,800 ingots, because the police had failed to prove that he had knowingly been dealing in stolen goods. Palmer, who had denied the charges, blew kisses to the jury on his way out of court. Most of the gold was never recovered but he did get that label, 'Goldfinger'.

At his later timeshare trial at the Old Bailey in 2002, the court was told that Palmer owned 'a confusing network of companies which pretended to be independent of each other'. The court also heard that tourists were subjected to high-pressure sales techniques after being approached on the streets of Tenerife. Thousands of ordinary people were tricked into buying timeshare apartments and handing over thousands of pounds in cash. The racket involved some 17,000 victims from all over Europe, with the largest group being British. Many were later targeted a second time when Palmer's companies offered to 'buy back' property, but first insisted on charging upfront for their services.

Palmer remained in the top 200 of *The Sunday Times* rich list for several years, even including the time he was in jail in the UK, until he fell off it in 2005. The previous year he had been at number 153, just behind the landowning Duke of Northumberland and EasyJet founder Stelios Haji-Ioannou.

Back in Tenerife, clear evidence of Palmer's 'kingdom' remains on the island. At the local marina, his 38-metre yacht *Brave Goose of Essex* is still fully staffed and on standby for Palmer at a moment's notice if he makes it back to the island one day. Then there are the eight properties he is said to still own on the island, not to mention another million pounds' worth of vintage cars in that lockup, on top of a rare red 'Gullwing' Mercedes.

During my visit to Tenerife I was introduced to a local fixer called Jamie, who actually worked for Palmer until the end of the 1990s. He was a mine of information about the way that Palmer and the other heavyweight Brit gangsters have been ruling this end of the island with a rod of iron for more than 20 years. 'A lot of these characters own the bars and the clubs and run the local brothels just to have businesses to launder their money through,' explained Jamie. He lives in a rented apartment right slap-bang in the middle of Playa de las Américas and claims he was often hired by British villains to carry out 'freelance' jobs on their behalf.

'I'm probably the only freelance out this way but I like it that way because it means no one owns me and orders me around,' he said. 'It also makes me seem more scary to the locals because they never know who exactly I'm working for at any one time.'

Jamie 'specialises' in debt collection, which seems to involve regular flashes of his gun in its shoulder holster. 'I'd never really use it, of course. I leave that to the fat, stupid lumps that work full time for the major faces round here. But I get a 40 per cent clawback from all the debts I collect, so the money can be pretty good at times because most of these debts are into the thousands, if not tens of thousands of euros.'

But Jamie then revealed a chilling story about another job he was hired to do, which seems to sum up the gang wars that are being waged out here in Tenerife. 'I was hired by the wealthy wife of a big name British gangster who was threatening to kill her because she had been having an affair with this gangster's best friend,' Jamie told me. 'This woman had heard of me on the grapevine and wanted someone she could trust to provide round-the-clock protection. She offered to pay me a fortune to look after her for a month until she flew back to the UK. I thought it was a bit strange that she didn't just go straight back to the UK but she was paying me so much dosh I chose not to ask any questions.'

Within 24 hours Jamie discovered exactly what was going on. 'It turned out that she was trying to finalise a massive coke deal with her husband's rival, who happened to be her lover as well. I was being hired as muscle to protect her from her nutter of a husband and, I can tell you, he was a big, mean nasty piece of work. I was well pissed off when I found out because I knew I'd be the first one in his gun sights if they came after her. Mind you, she was proving just as evil as her old man.

'I only found out all this when I was taking a break from protection duty while she was in her apartment screwing her boyfriend. I walked into a local bar and two lumps of meat came up to me and asked to have a word outside. I knew this was trouble but I didn't have much choice so I walked out to a car and got in and we had a chat.'

Jamie claims that one of the two men pulled a revolver out and pointed it straight at him. 'That's when they told me what she was up to. I immediately explained what had happened and for some weird reason they believed me and let me go. I actually think they wanted me to go back to her to give her a warning about everything. Well, I did exactly that and walked away from that job after talking to her. Three weeks later both those poor bastards who had talked to me in that bar were kidnapped by a bunch of rival Scousers and never seen again.'

Jamie says that the gang wars on Tenerife rarely get much attention beyond Playa de las Américas. 'It's almost as if we're being left to our own devices out here. The police and the authorities seem content just so long as we don't start shooting any innocent bystanders. It's a bit like a ghetto here. What goes in never usually comes out. But it means that feuds and stuff are dealt with quietly and efficiently. Meanwhile, all the normal residents try to just get on with their everyday lives as if nothing's happening. It's one hell of a weird place.'

In July 2006, six members of a British gang based in Playa de las Américas were charged with two attempted killings in a bloody feud between rival timeshare criminals. The men attacked two Lebanese businessmen on the holiday island as a vicious turf war between opposing salesmen spilled on to the streets of the resort.

Spanish police charged the gang with making threats of violence and attempted murder. It was alleged that the men, all aged between 26 and 40, had targeted their victims – brothers – following the break-up of a previous joint business venture. The arrests came as detectives in Tenerife were investigating links between the timeshare industry and extortion rackets being operated on the island by gangs of criminals.

Also in 2006, on the next door island of Gran Canaria, Spanish police arrested a suspected member of a Cuban-US criminal ring based in Florida and seized some €20 million (£18 million). The man, a 62-year-old Spanish national who was only identified by his name Leonardo AR, was at his home in the island capital of Las Palmas. He was charged together with his wife with money laundering for an organised crime gang known as 'The Corporation', whose leader, a US citizen of Cuban origin called José Battle, was already serving a 20-year-sentence in the US for criminal racketeering. Battle's son Miguel was also sentenced in the US to 15 years in prison for his role in criminal racketeering that included multiple murders and arson. The organisation had diverted to Spain large sums of money coming from tax havens in Panama.

So, while the Canaries may be as far from Spain as Britain is, it's clear that the influx of UK gangs means that crime travels far and wide.

GIBRALTAR

The Rock has become a centre for drug smuggling and money laundering

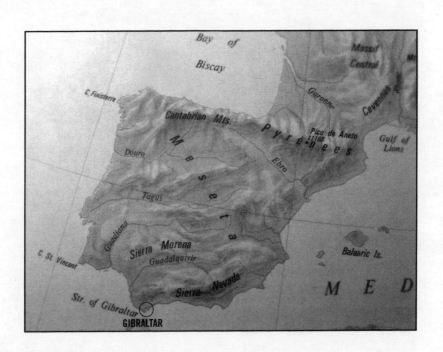

16

WELCOME TO THE Costa del Sol's controversial British-run neighbour. Gibraltar, or the Rock, is now used as a junction for hash from Morocco and cocaine from the Cali cartel in Columbia by many of Britain's most powerful gangs. The Spanish government reckons that Gibraltar's super-busy drug gangsters are importing more than a billion pounds' worth of narcotics each year right under the noses of this little piece of Britain on the armpit of the Mediterranean. Getting in and out of the Rock is so easy for gangsters that they've also turned Gibraltar into the money-laundering centre of the Europe.

Thin Phil – his real first name is every bit as clichéd – is a typical member of the Gibraltar Mafia. He works as a runner for a major former north London drug baron now based on the Rock. Thin Phil and other runners can make up to £5,000 a week steering their inflatables across the ocean. His boss has numerous boats, crews, lockups to store drugs, and dozens of people to load and unload his narcotics on both sides of the Strait.

The biggest earner used to be the hash available 23km due south in Morocco – a rich harvest of drugs less than an hour across a busy but under-policed stretch of water. However, these days the flotilla of speedboats and inflatables also smuggles other things. The biggest irony of all this is that while the British-run colony seems to be virtually turning a blind eye to these multimillion pound criminal enterprises, it's 'the fuckin' Spanish', as Thin Phil calls them, who are genuinely trying to crack down on this evil trade.

Spanish police now use a powerful launch – the smugglers call it a 'Turbo' – to pursue the drug couriers in their inflatables. And, naturally, they insist that Gibraltar's lawless reputation is yet more evidence that it should be permanently reunited with the Spanish mainland. In a community with only 30,000 inhabitants, nearly everyone on the Rock knows the men who work for the drug barons. Their tinted-window cars thud rap music out of rattling speakers as they coast up and down the colony's tacky high street, stuck in second gear. Yet they remain relatively untouched by the authorities.

Naturally, villains from the UK are drawn to the rock from their whitewashed villas on the Costa del Sol by the very Britishness of the place. Back in 2000, the then Spanish Prime Minister José María Aznar handed Tony Blair a file on alleged criminal activity on the Rock, which claimed that criminals – including at least six UK firms – on Gibraltar had begun turning their hand to murder and kidnappings connected to their big-money criminal enterprises.

Down at the Rock's Queensway Quay Marina, favourable mooring rates and luxurious amenities have even persuaded some of the Costa del Sol's flashier villains to keep their yachts tied up in Gibraltar when they are not out sailing the Med. Every now and again Gibraltar's puppet government is reminded by the big chiefs in Whitehall that they should crack down on the drug barons. Orders are issued to seize a few of the smugglers' favourite boats, the rigid inflatables. Then, as happened a few years back, the owners of these craft (the drug barons never have legally proven ownership) erupt, battle the police and cause a bit of mayhem.

The result? A discreet pause and then the boats are given back and business carries on as usual. The Rock's authorities even introduced a law banning any further importation of rigid inflatables. Owners of such boats were ordered to show evidence they were used for bona fide purposes. 'Now every inflatable owner has paperwork proving that he does boat trips for tourists,' says one Gibraltar regular. 'The law was a waste of time but at least it shut Whitehall up.'

Another important reason why so many British criminals use Gibraltar as a base for their dodgy enterprises is because the Rock is awash with 'funny money'. Of the £3.5 billion floating around Gibraltar (population: 30,000, registered companies: 35,000), more than half of it is reckoned to be the proceeds of illicit business dealings, smuggling and drug trafficking.

Back in the mid-nineties the US Drug Enforcement Agency and the British government set up Operation Dinero. Authorities created a fake offshore bank in the British dependency of Anguilla, which was then used by dozens of criminals and the majority of the cash that started being deposited was ... from Gibraltar. Offshore investors in the Rock have included such luminaries as pension-sapping newspaper baron Robert Maxwell and fraudster Peter Clowes of Barlow Clowes – a big player on the rock – who was convicted of diddling investors out of £150 million. Recently, Spanish authorities were horrified when they established links between the Basque separatist group ETA and money-laundering operations based in Gibraltar. They have no doubt the British-run colony is indirectly helping fund ETA bombings and killings in Spain.

One of the few Gibraltar-based gangsters to be actually nicked in recent years was Pasquale Locatelli, who used shipping companies based on the Rock to launder the proceeds of crime. Locatelli had connections with Rome Mafia boss Roberto Severa as well as Sicilian Mafia money man 'Pippo' Calo. Even Roberto Calvi, 'God's Banker', who was found hanging under Blackfriars Bridge after his bank slid into fraudulent bankruptcy in 1982, was linked to Locatelli and other Gibraltar-based individuals.

And then there is the latest money-obsessed boom to hit the Rock – gambling. While there is no suggestion that the spate of new betting enterprises is directly connected to criminals, gambling has made Gibraltar an even more attractive proposition to any Costa del Sol-based villain who fancies a flutter. In the past couple of years, Victor Chandler, Ladbrokes, Coral and Stan James have all set up betting operations from the Rock. They all insist that Gibraltar is ideal for them because of its favourable tax breaks, the English-speaking workforce and decent weather. 'Gibraltar is booming financially and a lot of it has to be down to the drug barons, money launderers and corrupt businesses,' says one former Gibraltar resident, Chris Coombes. 'If the UK tries to clean it up then it will rapidly slide into complete and utter financial collapse and that's when the Spanish will move in and make their strongest yet claim to rescue the colony.'

Spanish police divide the foreign criminal elements in Gibraltar into three groups: drug dealers who bring hashish and marijuana from Morocco; big organised crime gangs involved in extortion, kidnapping and contract killing; and, more recently, gangs from eastern Europe who break in and steal from luxury homes or purloin expensive cars.

In recent years killings between Gibraltar gangs have resulted in at least ten deaths. Only recently, a seven-year-old child and a male hairdresser were killed when two rival gangs fought a gun battle in a Marbella shopping arcade where the child was playing and the barber was working in his salon. Police said afterwards that the killings were linked to a Gibraltar drugs deal.

So it's not really surprising that in March 2005 one of Europe's largest money-laundering investigations by multiple police forces pointed the finger of suspicion at Gibraltar in a highly publicised case codenamed Operation Ballena Blanca (White Whale). It is estimated that at least €600 million was laundered through phantom companies and property deals using fictitious companies, many of which were based in Gibraltar.

The use of Gibraltar's offshore companies has long caused concern in Europe. Brussels recently gave Gibraltar five years to close down these phantom firms. Operation White Whale was sparked when French police requested information on a Spanish-based company, which was believed to be involved in drug trafficking. It was during these investigations that a much wider network of criminality emerged. In total, 41 people, including lawyers and public notaries, were detained for questioning. The detainees were British, French, Dutch, Finnish, Moroccan, Russian and Ukrainian.

In a series of raids along the nearby Costa del Sol, stretching from Málaga to Sotogrande near Gibraltar, authorities confiscated 251 properties, including two entire housing developments – one finished and one still under construction – and 42 Rolls-Royce, Ferrari, Porsche and Mercedes cars. There also took other vehicles plus a yacht, two private planes, quad bikes, jewellery, Picasso and Miró paintings, bank accounts and cash.

The Russian gangs have already got a violent toehold in the nearby Costa del Sol but these days they have been increasingly using Gibraltar as an illegal haven for cash and dodgy business transactions. One Marbella lawyer told me he had regularly handled property purchases from Russian clients who paid with suitcases full of US dollars. There were even suspicions that the Russian oil company, Yukos, recently taken over by the state, could have even been using Gibraltar to launder its ill-gotten gains.

Back in 1999, when Spain's then prime minister, José María Aznar, alleged that Gibraltar-based criminal gangs were behind everything from drug trafficking and money laundering to murder and kidnapping, it provoked outrage in Gibraltar. Local authorities claimed it was part of a Spanish smear campaign. But the Spanish report highlighted how 12 Gibraltar-based vessels had been caught trafficking drugs in Spanish waters the previous year. It also listed four major police operations in which large quantities of hashish, cocaine and designer drugs such as ecstasy had been captured, and revealed details of a Gibraltar gang that was behind every form of organised crime 'not discounting murder or kidnap'.

The chief minister of Gibraltar, Peter Caruana, expressed outrage at the Spanish allegations. 'I have never before been accused of complicity or tolerance of kidnapping and murder,' he said indignantly.

Spain even accused Gibraltar of costing Spain €6 billion in lost tax revenue every year and said that its laws failed to comply with more than 50 EU directives. British officials insist that money laundering on such a scale is impossible and that Gibraltar has a better record in meeting EU directives than Spain.

But there is absolutely no doubt that the gangs are continuing to thrive on the Rock. Despite the worldwide recession biting hard, increasing numbers of shadowy figures are using Gibraltar to hide their proceeds from crime and its place as the centre of dodgy dealings seems assured for many years to come.

CONCLUSION

Gangster John Palmer's timeshare empire on Tenerife.

GANGS ARE UNDOUBTEDLY stepping up their criminal activities in Spain as the worldwide recession bites. In September 2008, police across Spain arrested 18 members of a gang from Albania and Serbia and Montenegro's Kosovo, who had committed robberies of houses and commercial ships. Gang members were detained in Barcelona, Cádiz, Granada, Madrid and Valencia and accused of being involved in 77 robberies. The gang used sophisticated alarm-disabling equipment, night-vision goggles, chisels, maces, torches, gloves and walkie-talkies in their raids. They also organised a large network of lodgings and vehicles, which allowed them to change their centre of operations at regular intervals to avoid being caught.

The involvement of foreigners and organised criminals in Spain has underscored the need for close cooperation between European law-enforcement officials. Local authorities have tried to ignore or downplay the amount of violent activity on the coastal regions in order not to discourage tourism.

A classic example of a violent yet professional group of criminals was the legendary Nose Gang, a group of Italians accused of bank robberies and kidnapping. The name 'Nose

Gang' was attributed to the members' use of clownish false noses as disguises while they robbed banks. They were also charged with kidnappings in France and Italy, cutting off their victims' ears and sending them to their families. The Nose Gang hit small Spanish cities such as Albacete, Salamanca and Zamora, terrorising bank staff and customers alike while getting away with half a million pounds in cash and the contents of numerous safe deposit boxes.

One attempt by the gang to rob a bank in Córdoba was foiled when traffic police towed away the robbers' getaway car. As the gang stole another car and tried to flee they machine-gunned two policewomen, who died. A hostage was seriously injured. When police finally arrested the robbers, they uncovered an arsenal of weapons, including an automatic assault rifle, three Browning pistols and two Colt .45s.

Europol, the European Union's police office, has warned governments of a clear and present threat from transnational gangs trafficking in arms, drugs and people, as well as running counterfeiting and money-laundering rackets. The bottom line is that cross-border crime is on the rise across Europe. These gangs are exploiting the lowering of national trade and travel barriers to commit crimes and escape punishment.

So it is clear that many dangerous gangs have established a foothold in Spain. The upsurge in gang activity has coincided with the high tide of immigration during the economic boom in the 1990s. Spain's immigrant population has more than tripled since 2000. According to Madrid city statistics, one out of every six of its three million inhabitants is now foreign-born, and non-natives currently account for 9.9 per cent of the country's 45 million people, up from 2.3 per cent in 2000.

As mentioned earlier in this book, € 500 notes are known in Spain as 'Bin Ladens' because, like the elusive leader of al-Qaeda, everyone knows the notes exist but they are rarely, if ever, seen. But Spain has in recent years been swamped by these purple notes, which are used by organised-crime gangs to launder money gained from drug dealing, extortion, people smuggling and prostitution. In the past year the number of € 500 (£475) notes in circulation in Spain has risen by 36 per cent to 95 million, according to the Bank of Spain. In theory, that's two € 500 notes for every one of the 44 million people living in the country. In fact, only a tiny number of people ever see these notes.

Analysts have called for more checks on who is requesting these notes. The Bank of Spain and other banks have been criticised for not asking questions when they are asked to provide these notes. A quarter of all the € 500 notes in Europe are circulating in Spain. In 2006, an international police operation led to the arrest of 47 people, including two Britons, in Marbella on the Costa del Sol, in connection with an alleged € 250 million money-laundering scam.

Criminals often evade alerting the authorities in banks by making multiple payments of up to € 2,999 in cash at a time – the total amount that bank customers can pay without identifying themselves. Tax authorities are alarmed by the amount of revenue being lost to the Spanish government because of lax controls and insufficient resources to confront the fraudsters. Experts estimate that almost a quarter of Spain's GDP – or €130 billion – is never declared. That means Spain has the second-highest level of fraud, through undeclared transactions, in Europe, after Greece.

Disturbingly, the Guardia Civil insist they simply do not have the resources to check each of the 20,000 Interpol inquiries received annually concerning British criminals being sought in Spain. It's not surprising, therefore, that certain British gangs continue to widen their operations in Spain. In October 2006 police from Britain and Spain began a campaign to round up fugitives hiding on the Costas, amid concerns that Spain was still the number-one destination for runaway UK criminals. Operation Captura aimed to disrupt criminal networks. The Serious Organised Crime Agency continues to identify Spain as an important base for British criminals directing international drug-trafficking networks.

Those sought by British police in Spain included escaped prisoners, murder suspects, drug traffickers, fraudsters, counterfeiters and robbery suspects. A hotline was even set up in Spain for British expatriates to call with anonymous tips on the whereabouts of the so-called top ten people listed on the 'Crimestoppers Costas' website.

Some of the alleged criminals listed were wanted for extremely serious crimes. Police to this day are offering a reward of up to £30,000 for information leading to the arrest and imprisonment of James Francis Hurley, a convicted murderer and armed robber who escaped during a prison transfer in 1994. Hurley was convicted of shooting a policeman to death during a bank robbery in Hemel Hempstead. Others being sought include Christopher Guest More, wanted in connection with the kidnap and murder of a man in 2003, and Mark Gottfried, wanted on drug trafficking charges and for impersonating a Customs officer.

So, the overall picture is grim. It seems that the gang wars on the Costas are here to stay. The Spanish and UK police are virtually impotent, unable to stretch their meagre resources to make anything other than a very small dent in the criminal enterprises that continue to fuel Spain's coastal economy to this day.

In this book you have met murderers, rapists, drug dealers, pimps, people smugglers and counterfeiters. I've encountered men with gunshot and knife wounds and those whose wives or girlfriends have been kidnapped and raped by rival gangs. This is the reality of Spain as this decade comes to a close.

Just days before completing this book, yet another deadly incident highlighting the gang wars on the Costas occurred. In January 2009, Irish and Romanian gangs exchanged gunfire in the run-down resort area of Benalmadena on the Costa del Sol in another turf war on this tatty stretch of coastline, which has been turned into a virtual desert town by the crippling financial recession sweeping the globe.

In among the tower blocks of Benalmadena are numerous young kids for whom gang membership is their ultimate ambition. They hear the stories about the drugs, the robberies, the violence, the killings and the rivalry and it feeds them a twisted dream. Many of these kids have been brought up on a TV diet of 'gangsta', featuring rap artists telling the world how they shot down their enemies.

Spain has proved to be Europe's ultimate criminal melting pot and the Brits are still right there in the centre of things, even though they are being rivalled by the even more cold-blooded foreign gangs from as far away as eastern Europe and South America.

I've been surprised by the level of access I've been able to gain to some of these gangs for this book. Many of the older faces have been surprised that I managed to get any of the younger 'cowboys' to open up but it seems that many are extremely proud of their 'activities'. In other words, they cannot resist showing off because they want to be *somebody*. It may also have something to do with their consumption of cocaine and other drugs because it seems to have made many of these younger gangsters far more reckless than a lot of their predecessors. Yet a few of these drug-fuelled hoods have shown a surprising amount of humility. They are not all simply cold-blooded desperados prepared to kill anyone to get what they want. Far from it – many are just lost souls, abandoned by their families at an early age and left to fend for themselves. It's not really so surprising they opted for a life of crime. They had little choice.

Crime used to thrive in the poorest areas but these days the spider's net is widening more and more. As the global financial meltdown bites, it is expected that many of these gangs will push deeper and deeper into the areas that most law-abiding citizens presume to be safe for themselves and their families. Desperation will undoubtedly (and already is in some cases) bringing with it more danger to innocent people as the gangs find it harder to make money from traditional criminal sources.

Many of the police I have talked to in Spain believe that there will be an increase in kidnapping throughout the country. They say it is inevitable that the gangs will start to target the very rich because this is one crime that the victims' families rarely want to report to the police out of fear. In places like Colombia, kidnappings have long since become a national criminal pastime. With drug prices collapsing and other more traditional underworld enterprises such as people-smuggling and prostitution also suffering thanks to the financial crisis, the very rich will become the most obvious targets.

Yet one must never overlook the fact that the gangs who are contributing so much to Spain's economy have been virtually encouraged by a government that for so many years chose to ignore the so-called 'black economy'. Under

Franco, Spain tempted millions of tourists to visit and even refused to extradite the criminals from Britain who first made their homes on the Costas. Dictator Franco knew only too well that anyone's cash, even that belonging to criminals, was worth having.

That attitude pervaded long after Franco's death more than 30 years ago and there is absolutely no doubt that to a certain degree it has helped prop up Spain's economy ever since. But this country is now entering a new, even more dangerous phase. The worldwide economic meltdown has hit Spain worse than any other country in Europe. That means there simply isn't enough money or work to go round. The criminals themselves are struggling to make ends meet and this is having a knock-on effect, especially in the mainly crime-driven coastal areas.

The idea behind this book was to expose the reality of what is really going on close to the beaches where millions of holidaymakers sunbathe every year. If only they knew just how much criminal activity was happening literally on their doorstep.

In a perfect world, criminals would have no crimes to commit and everyone would live in peace and harmony. But obviously it just doesn't work like that. I doubt if *Gang Wars on the Costa* is going to make much difference to Spain's crime problem, but it's important to highlight what is going on. More and more young people are interested in the gangs and how they operate. And these are not just the young hoods living in the sprawling concrete jungles of

Benalmadena. Many are middle-class kids with a genuine interest in what is happening in the world. They are worried about their futures, because at this rate the gangs are going to dominate the streets even more in the future. They are increasingly going to start coming out from the shadows as the poorly paid police struggle to keep law and order.

I have in the past been accused of glorifying criminals. No doubt some in their safe white ivory towers miles away from the criminal hinterlands on the Costas will accuse me of exaggerating about the underworld but I can assure you this book only covers the tip of the criminal iceberg. The only conclusion I can reach after writing and researching this subject is that the gap between the rich and the poor is going to get even wider over the next few years. As the world becomes gripped by increasing poverty, the gangs will recruit more members. I predict that older disaffected people, some even in their sixties, will start to form unofficial gangs in order to create their own 'families' in just the same way younger people have been doing for centuries. With depleted pensions many will seek solace in each other's company because of their enforced poverty. As the number of single people increases and the finances of the elderly worsen, they will be faced with little choice but to join forces with others in a similar predicament.

That means we could have a situation where pensioner gangs may really pose a threat. Don't laugh. It's a serious prediction and it makes total sense. I am not saying these gangs of old people will be out on the streets mugging and pillaging but they will exist because people need to belong. And if their families have disintegrated and they are virtually penniless then they will join forces with other like-minded people. One veteran south London bank robber – now settled in Spain – told me recently that a lot of his criminal associates were getting increasingly bored and lonely in old age. 'They need to belong to a club and that's what a gang is in a sense,' this old-timer told me. 'Just imagine the brain power if we all got together. We wouldn't make the same mistakes we did when we were younger. We could pull off some stunning jobs and probably get away with it much more than we used to.'

It's a bizarre thought isn't it? Gangs of pensioner criminals masterminding heists and drug deals from the safety of their Zimmer frames. Well not quite. But on a serious level it will happen eventually. There is no doubt about it. Let's face it – part of the reason people join gangs is for the friendship, loyalty and respect they cannot find anywhere else. Others simply want to steal and break the law because they think it's easier than leading a 'straight' life. But as one British gang member in southern Spain told me, 'No one in their right mind would chose to be a criminal. It's a hard life and there's no pension at the end of it, just a lot of stress. It may be the oldest cliché in the book but crime really doesn't pay. Believe me. I know that for a fact.'

So overall, it looks as if the gang wars in Spain are set to grow into an even bigger problem as the world goes through the financial recession. As previously mentioned, the police will struggle in their fight against crime as people's finances crash around them.

In Spain, many believe society will slip back into being more like the Third World country it was until 25 years ago. Inland, the rural communities will fend for themselves while the once rich and flashy coastal regions will crumble into disrepair. Standards will drop and the jobs that are fuelled by tourism will collapse, leaving huge numbers out of work.

Ironically, in Spain it might actually mean a return to the sort of family values that used to dominate this once strict Catholic society. Many will have no choice but to go back to their families in the *campo* (countryside) and try to survive off the land. The good thing about this is that there will be less for the gangs to steal, which might mean in the long run there is an outside chance that they may not thrive and could even start to fade out altogether. But that is projecting a long way into the future. It's more likely they will thrive on the poverty and desperation of others in the way they always have in the more traditionally poor nations of the world.

Whatever happens, there is no doubt that Spain is paying a terrible price for having turned a blind eye for so long to these bandits and their criminal habits...

POSTSCRIPT

SHORTLY AFTER COMPLETING this book, I got a call from two Costa Blanca British gangsters called Jim and Tel, who helped me when I was on a research trip in their 'manor', just south of Benidorm. They'd both moved back to the UK in recent weeks because there was no 'work' for them back in Spain. Their 'speciality' had been smuggling cocaine and cannabis on small yachts across the Mediterranean. Both Jim and Tel had spent ten years on the Costa Blanca but, in their words, 'there's nothing left there. The place is like a desert. It had become impossible to make any money, straight or crooked.'

In recent years, Jim and Tel had also 'specialised' in mortgage fraud when their drug running trips became less frequent. At one stage, they'd owned a highly profitable chain of estate agents on the Costa Blanca. Jim explained: 'That estate agency business was like a licence to print money back when properties were selling like hot cakes and we put all our drug money through it as well.'

But the two old mates had reluctantly decided to quit Spain just before Christmas 2008. Explained Tel: 'It wasn't easy turning our backs on all that sunshine but the quality of life in Spain was disappearing fast. At least back here people still have the money to buy a few drugs and go out and have a good time. I just look back on those days in Spain as being a right laugh but now its back to reality here in the UK.'

And Jim had one word of advice for anyone planning to head out to Spain to start a new life. 'Don't bother. There's nothing there for anyone. The good times have gone and everyone in Spain is going to have it harder than anywhere else in Europe. They've had all these massive injections of cash from the EEC but what have they got to show for it? *Fuck all.'*

AUTHOR'S NOTE

TO ALL THE characters I've encountered on my travels in Spain I offer my eternal gratitude. Many of them have chosen not to be fully identified because of the very gang wars that I have highlighted in this book. That is their choice and I fully respect it. I'd also like to thank the good, law-abiding citizens of Spain who've endured many difficult periods in their turbulent history over the last 100 years. I am sure they will recover from the recession, which is tearing their wonderful country apart. I am only sorry that they've been inflicted with so many bad Britons along the way.

Most of the dialogue used here was drawn from actual interviews. Some was reconstructed from available documents; a few descriptions were reconstituted from the memory of others. There are no hidden agendas in these stories, and I make no apology for the strong language.

Wensley Clarkson
Spain, 2009

MORE OF SPAIN'S MOST NOTORIOUS BRITS

James HURLEY – convicted killer of a policeman who escaped custody in 1994. He was arrested in 2007 in The Netherlands for drug offences.

Ian WHITE – tobacco smuggler who masterminded a £6 million VAT scam, arrested in Spain. He was tried, convicted and sentenced to six years imprisonment in his absence on the 11th March 2004. He was returned to the UK on the 20th September 2007 and after appearing in court he was sent to prison to start serving his sentence.

Anthony SIMMONDS – wanted for importing large quantities of cannabis from Spain and cheating VAT of £4 million. Arrested in Spain in December 2006 and was returned to the UK in early 2007. After appearing in court his sentence of three years' imprisonment was confirmed. He was also given a three-month sentence in respect of the absconding, which is being served consecutively.

Clifford HOBBS – escaped in custody on his way to court in London where he was to stand trial for the theft of £1.25 million from a security van. Arrested in Spain and returned to the UK in August 2007. Hobbs was jailed at Woolwich Crown Court in February 2008 for 12 years for possession of a firearm and 7 years for his escape (both sentences to run concurrently). He was also sentenced to 6 years for conspiracy to steal.

Dante LATRECHE – wanted for credit card fraud. Arrested in UK in 2007 and has received suspended prison sentence.

John DOWDALL - wanted for importing large quantities of cannabis from Spain in 2003. He was tried, convicted and sentenced to five years' imprisonment in his absence on the 17th May 2005. After being arrested in Spain, he was returned to the UK in September 2007. After appearing in court he was sentenced to a further four months' imprisonment, which is to run consecutively to the sentence of his original sentence.

Markcus JAMAL – wanted for conspiracy for murder of Nageeb El Hakem in 2005. He was arrested in Spain and returned to the UK in January 2007. He was sentenced that year to an indefinite term (which is almost identical to a life sentence) but had that reduced, after an appeal, to 22 years.

John SETON – wanted for the murder of Garage owner Jon Bartlett in March 2006. Arrested in the Netherlands and returned to the UK in May 2007. In September 2008, after pleading not guilty, he was imprisoned for life.

Donald HAISMAN – wanted for drug offences and arrested in Belgium in February 2008.

Lisa SANDERSON – Wanted for obtaining property mortgages by deception (three offences in total, jointly with seven others with a total monetary value of £1.2 million). She was arrested in Portugal in September 2008.

Robert SPIERS – was wanted in connection with a shooting in a UK public house, He was arrested in Spain in July 2008 after being on the run for two years.

James GULLIFORD - On 30 April 2003 it is alleged that Gulliford stabbed another man with a screwdriver over a suspected drugs debt. He was arrested in Spain in January 2008.

John Cearney BARKER - Barker was wanted under two European Arrest Warrants for trafficking in cocaine and amphetamine to the value of over £110,000 in 1998 and 1999 within Scotland. He was arrested in Spain early in 2008.